The Gospel of Matthew

 The Illustrated
International Children's Bible®

Design and Illustration from
Neely Publishing LLC.

Individual contributors:
Keith R. Neely, David Miles, Roberta Neely,
Bridget Harlow and Thomas R. Zuber

Tommy NELSON

A Division of Thomas Nelson Publishers
Since 1798

www.TommyNelson.com
a division of
Thomas Nelson, Inc.
www.thomasnelson.com

Introduction

Welcome! You've just picked up one of the most amazing books of all time, the Holy Bible. This book of the Bible, Matthew, is presented in a way that has never been done before. Want to know how and why we've done it this way? Keep reading to find out!

Our Purpose
We did not want to create just another children's Bible storybook. In other words, we didn't want to have Bible pictures alongside words that are a retelling of God's Word, the Holy Scriptures. We wanted to draw attention to, magnify, and clarify the actual Word of God. In those words lies the power to change the lives of children and adults alike!

"God's word is alive and working." Hebrews 4:12

"But the word of the Lord will live forever." 1 Peter 1:25

In the same way that written illustrations or "word pictures" are used to help make an idea easy to understand and memorable, our visual illustrations will make the actual Word of God easier to understand than ever before.

The Illustrated International Children's Bible®
The International Children's Bible® was the first translation created especially for children. It has been illustrated in a frame-by-frame format style. These realistic images help illustrate the actual Scriptures . . . the events of the Bible. The format helps to carry the reader easily through each story like a visual movie. This not only makes the verses easier to understand, but also easier to memorize!

Actual Scriptures: Yes, that's right . . . the pages of this book are actual Bible verses. On some pages you'll see the characters speaking by the use of a dialog box. The action and setting of the scene is readily apparent by the backgrounds. What a great way to read and learn your Bible! Some of the verses are not a person speaking, so they will be in plain boxes. You might see some small "d's" in the text. These indicate a word that will have a definition in the dictionary found at the back of full ICB Bibles.

Old Testament quotations are shown in a separate treatment. They are in a parchment like background to represent that they are older words, almost like a treasured antique. They will usually have the book, chapter, and verse with them so you can know where they came from in the Old Testament.

> 5 "Tell the people of Jerusalem, 'Your king is coming to you. He is gentle and riding on a donkey. He is on the colt of a donkey.' "
>
> *Zechariah 9:9*

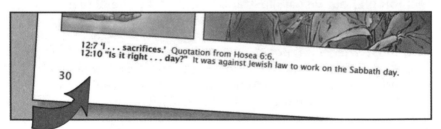

Footnotes appear at the bottom of some pages. They are represented in the Bible verses by a small "n." That will let you know that there is a note at the bottom of the page that gives you a little more information about that word or phrase. Just more information that's helpful to know!

In some chapters and verses there will not be a lot of interaction between Bible characters, but you will see background scenery, maps, and other interesting treatments to help make your Bible reading more fun and helpful. Most Bible storybooks are just that . . . stories retold to make them easier to understand. Never before has actual Bible Scripture been illustrated in this form so that children and adults can immediately read and know what is going on in a certain verse–who was talking, what time of day it was, was it inside or out, who was there. We hope you enjoy reading this Bible and have fun learning along the way!

The Publishers

Look for these other titles coming soon.

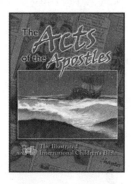
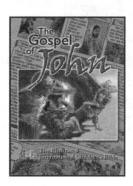
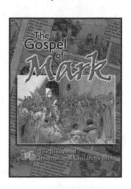

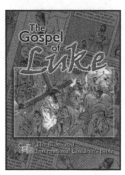

and

Table of Contents

The
Gospel
of
Matthew

Matthew chapter 1

Matthew Tells About Jesus the King of the Jews

The Family History of Jesus

1 This is the family history of Jesus Christ. He came from the family of David. David came from the family of Abraham. 2 Abraham was the father[n] of Isaac. Isaac was the father of Jacob. Jacob was the father of Judah and his brothers. 3 Judah was the father of Perez and Zerah. (Their mother was Tamar.) Perez was the father of Hezron. Hezron was the father of Ram. 4 Ram was the father of Amminadab. Amminadab was the father of Nahshon. Nahshon was the father of Salmon. 5 Salmon was the father of Boaz. (Boaz's mother was Rahab.) Boaz was the father of Obed. (Obed's mother was Ruth.) Obed was the father of Jesse. 6 Jesse was the father of King David. David was the father of Solomon. (Solomon's mother had been Uriah's wife.) 7 Solomon was the father of Rehoboam. Rehoboam was the father of Abijah. Abijah was the father of Asa.[n] 8 Asa was the father of Jehoshaphat. Jehoshaphat was the father of Jehoram. Jehoram was the ancestor of Uzziah. 9 Uzziah was the father of Jotham. Jotham was the father of Ahaz. Ahaz was the father of Hezekiah. 10 Hezekiah was the father of Manasseh. Manasseh was the father of Amon. Amon was the father of Josiah. 11 Josiah was the grandfather of Jehoiachin[n] and his brothers. (This was at the time that the people were taken to Babylon.) 12 After they were taken to Babylon: Jehoiachin was the father of Shealtiel. Shealtiel was the grandfather of Zerubbabel. 13 Zerubbabel was the father of Abiud. Abiud was the father of Eliakim. Eliakim was the father of Azor. 14 Azor was the father of Zadok. Zadok was the father of Akim. Akim was the father of Eliud. 15 Eliud was the father of Eleazar. Eleazar was the father of Matthan. Matthan was the father of Jacob. 16 Jacob was the father of Joseph. Joseph was the husband of Mary, and Mary was the mother of Jesus. Jesus is called the Christ.[d] 17 So there were 14 generations from Abraham to David. And there were 14 generations from David until the time when the people were taken to Babylon. And there were 14 generations from the time when the people were taken to Babylon until Christ was born.

The Birth of Jesus Christ

18 The mother of Jesus Christ was Mary. And this is how the birth of Jesus came about. Mary was engaged to marry Joseph. But before they married, she learned that she was going to have a baby. She was pregnant by the power of the Holy Spirit.[d] 19 Mary's husband, Joseph, was a good man. He did not want to disgrace her in public, so he planned to divorce her secretly.

1:2 father "Father" in Jewish lists of ancestors can sometimes mean grandfather or more distant relative. **1:7 Asa** Some Greek Copies read "Asaph," another name for Asa (see 1 Chronicles 3:10). **1:11 Jehoiachin** The Greek reads "Jeconiah," another name for Jehoiachin (see 2 Kings 24:6 and 1 Chronicles 3:16).

20 While Joseph thought about this, an angel of the Lord came to him in a dream. The angel said,

"Joseph, descendant[d] of David, don't be afraid to take Mary as your wife. The baby in her is from the Holy Spirit. 21 She will give birth to a son. You will name the son Jesus.[n] Give him that name because he will save his people from their sins."

22 All this happened to make clear the full meaning of what the Lord had said through the prophet:[d] 23 "The virgin[d] will be pregnant. She will have a son, and they will name him Immanuel."[n] This name means "God is with us."

24 When Joseph woke up, he did what the Lord's angel had told him to do. Joseph married Mary.

25 But he did not have sexual relations with her until she gave birth to the son. And Joseph named the son Jesus.

Chapter 2

Wise Men Come to Visit Jesus

1 Jesus was born in the town of Bethlehem in Judea during the time when Herod was king. After Jesus was born, some wise men from the east came to Jerusalem. 2 They asked,

"Where is the baby who was born to be the king of the Jews? We saw his star in the east. We came to worship him."

1:21 **Jesus** The name Jesus means "salvation."
1:23 **"The virgin . . . Immanuel."** Quotation from Isaiah 7:14.

3 When King Herod heard about this new king of the Jews, he was troubled. And all the people in Jerusalem were worried too. 4 Herod called a meeting of all the leading priests and teachers of the law. He asked them where the Christ[d] would be born. 5 They answered,

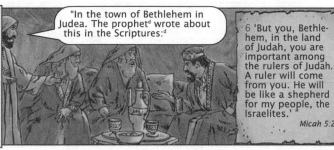

"In the town of Bethlehem in Judea. The prophet[d] wrote about this in the Scriptures:[d]

6 'But you, Bethlehem, in the land of Judah, you are important among the rulers of Judah. A ruler will come from you. He will be like a shepherd for my people, the Israelites.' "

Micah 5:2

7 Then Herod had a secret meeting with the wise men from the east. He learned from them the exact time they first saw the star. 8 Then Herod sent the wise men to Bethlehem. He said to them,

"Go and look carefully to find the child. When you find him, come tell me. Then I can go worship him too."

9 The wise men heard the king and then left. They saw the same star they had seen in the east. It went before them until it stopped above the place where the child was. 10 When the wise men saw the star, they were filled with joy. 11 They went to the house where the child was and saw him with his mother, Mary. They bowed down and worshiped the child.

They opened the gifts they brought for him. They gave him treasures of gold, frankincense,[d] and myrrh.[d]

12 But God warned the wise men in a dream not to go back to Herod. So they went home to their own country by a different way.

Jesus' Parents Take Him to Egypt

13 After they left, an angel of the Lord came to Joseph in a dream. The angel said,

"Get up! Take the child and his mother and escape to Egypt. Herod will start looking for the child to kill him. Stay in Egypt until I tell you to return."

14 So Joseph got up and left for Egypt during the night with the child and his mother.

Matthew 2:15-23

15 Joseph stayed in Egypt until Herod died. This was to make clear the full meaning of what the Lord had said through the prophet.[d] The Lord said, "I called my son out of Egypt."[n]

Herod Kills the Baby Boys

16 When Herod saw that the wise men had tricked him, he was very angry.

So he gave an order to kill all the baby boys in Bethlehem and in all the area around Bethlehem who were two years old or younger. This was in keeping with the time he learned from the wise men.

17 So what God had said through the prophet[d] Jeremiah came true:

18 "A sound was heard in Ramah. It was painful crying and much sadness. Rachel cries for her children, and she cannot be comforted, because her children are dead." *Jeremiah 31:15*

Joseph and Mary Return

19 After Herod died, an angel of the Lord came to Joseph in a dream. This happened while Joseph was in Egypt. 20 The angel said,

"Get up! Take the child and his mother and go to Israel. The people who were trying to kill the child are now dead."

21 So Joseph took the child and his mother and went to Israel. 22 But he heard that Archelaus was now king in Judea. Archelaus became king when his father Herod died. So Joseph was afraid to go there. After being warned in a dream, he went to the area of Galilee.

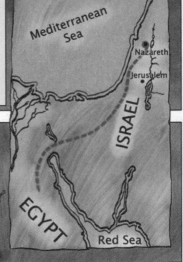

Mediterranean Sea

Nazareth

Jerusalem

ISRAEL

EGYPT

Red Sea

23 He went to a town called Nazareth and lived there. And so what God had said through the prophets[d] came true: "He will be called a Nazarene."[n]

2:15 "I called . . . Egypt." Quotation from Hosea 11:1. **2:23 Nazarene** A person from the town of Nazareth. Matthew may be referring to Isaiah 11:1, where the Hebrew word translated "branch" sounds like "Nazarene."

Chapter

3

The Work of
John the Baptist

1 About that time John the Baptist^d came and began preaching in the desert area of Judea. 2 John said,

"Change your hearts and lives because the kingdom of heaven is coming soon."

3 John the Baptist is the one Isaiah the prophet^d was talking about. Isaiah said:

"This is a voice of a man who calls out in the desert: 'Prepare the way for the Lord. Make the road straight for him.' "
Isaiah 40:3

4 John's clothes were made from camel's hair. He wore a leather belt around his waist. For food, he ate locusts^d and wild honey. 5 Many people went to hear John preach. They came from Jerusalem and all Judea and all the area around the Jordan River. 6 They told of the sins they had done, and John baptized them in the Jordan River. 7 Many of the Pharisees^d and Sadducees^d came to the place where John was baptizing people. When John saw them, he said:

Matthew 3:8-17

"You are snakes! Who warned you to run away from God's anger that is coming?

8 You must do the things that show that you have really changed your hearts and lives. 9 And don't think that you can say to yourselves,

'Abraham is our father.' I tell you that God could make children for Abraham from these rocks.

10 The ax is now ready to cut down the trees. Every tree that does not produce good fruit will be cut down and thrown into the fire.[n]
11 "I baptize you with water to show that your hearts and lives have changed. But there is one coming later who is greater than I am. I am not good enough to carry his sandals. He will baptize you with the Holy Spirit[d] and with fire. 12 He will come ready to clean the grain. He will separate the good grain from the chaff.[d] He will put the good part of the grain into his barn. And he will burn the chaff with a fire that cannot be put out."[n]

Jesus Is Baptized by John

13 At that time Jesus came from Galilee to the Jordan River. He came to John and wanted John to baptize him.

14 But John tried to stop him. John said,

"Why do you come to me to be baptized? I should be baptized by you!"

15 Jesus answered,

"Let it be this way for now. We should do all things that are right."

So John agreed to baptize Jesus.

16 Jesus was baptized and came up out of the water. Heaven opened, and he saw God's Spirit[d] coming down on him like a dove. 17 And a voice spoke from heaven. The voice said,

"This is my Son and I love him. I am very pleased with him."

3:10 The ax . . . fire. This means that God is ready to punish his people who do not obey him. **3:12 He will . . . out.** This means that Jesus will come to separate the good people from the bad people, saving the good and punishing the bad.

Chapter 4

The Temptation of Jesus

1 Then the Spirit[d] led Jesus into the desert to be tempted by the devil.

2 Jesus ate nothing for 40 days and nights. After this, he was very hungry. 3 The devil came to Jesus to tempt him. The devil said,

"If you are the Son of God, tell these rocks to become bread."

4 Jesus answered,

"It is written in the Scriptures[d] 'A person does not live only by eating bread. But a person lives by everything the Lord says.'"[n]

5 Then the devil led Jesus to the holy city of Jerusalem. He put Jesus on a very high place of the Temple.[d] 6 The devil said,

"If you are the Son of God, jump off. It is written in the Scriptures, 'He has put his angels in charge of you. They will catch you with their hands. And you will not hit your foot on a rock.'"
Psalm 91:11-12

7 Jesus answered him,

"It also says in the Scriptures, 'Do not test the Lord your God.'"[n]

8 Then the devil led Jesus to the top of a very high mountain. He showed Jesus all the kingdoms of the world and all the great things that are in those kingdoms. 9 The devil said,

"If you will bow down and worship me, I will give you all these things."

10 Jesus said to the devil,

"Go away from me, Satan! It is written in the Scriptures, 'You must worship the Lord your God. Serve only him!'"[n]

4:4 'A person . . . says.' Quotation from Deuteronomy 8:3.
4:7 'Do . . . God.' Quotation from Deuteronomy 6:16.
4:10 'You . . . him!' Quotation from Deuteronomy 6:13.

11 So the devil left Jesus. And then some angels came to Jesus and helped him.

Jesus Begins Work in Galilee

12 Jesus heard that John had been put in prison. So Jesus went back to Galilee. 13 He left Nazareth and went and lived in Capernaum, a town near Lake Galilee. Capernaum is in the area near Zebulun and Naphtali. 14 Jesus did this to make true what the prophet[d] Isaiah said:

15 "Land of Zebulun and land of Naphtali are on the way to the sea. They are along the Jordan River. This is Galilee where the non-Jewish people live. 16 These people who live in darkness will see a great light. They live in a place that is very dark. But a light will shine on them."

Isaiah 9:1-2

Jesus Chooses Some Followers

17 From that time Jesus began to preach, saying,

"Change your hearts and lives, because the kingdom of heaven is coming soon."

Mediterranean Sea

Galilee

Capernum

NAPHTALI — SEA OF GALILEE

Nazareth

ZEBULUN

Jordan River

DEAD SEA

18 Jesus was walking by Lake Galilee. He saw two brothers, Simon (called Peter) and Simon's brother Andrew. The brothers were fishermen, and they were fishing in the lake with a net. 19 Jesus said,

"Come follow me. I will make you fishermen for men."

20 At once Simon and Andrew left their nets and followed him.
21 Jesus continued walking by Lake Galilee. He saw two other brothers, James and John, the sons of Zebedee. They were in a boat with their father Zebedee, preparing their nets to catch fish. Jesus told them to come with him. 22 At once they left the boat and their father, and they followed Jesus.

Jesus Teaches and Heals People

23 Jesus went everywhere in Galilee. He taught in the synagogues[d] and preached the Good News[d] about the kingdom of heaven. And he healed all the people's diseases and sicknesses. 24 The news about Jesus spread all over Syria, and people brought all the sick to him. These sick people were suffering from different kinds of diseases and pain. Some were suffering very great pain, some had demons,[d] some were epileptics,[n] and some were paralyzed. Jesus healed all of them. 25 Many people followed him. They came from Galilee, the Ten Towns,[n] Jerusalem, Judea, and the land across the Jordan River.

Chapter

5

Jesus Teaches the People

1 Jesus saw the crowds who were there.

4:24 epileptics People with a disease that causes them sometimes to lose control of their bodies, and maybe faint, shake strongly, or not be able to move. **4:25 Ten Towns** In Greek, called "Decapolis." It was an area east of Lake Galilee that once had ten main towns.

Matthew 5:2-15

He went up on a hill and sat down. His followers came to him. 2 Jesus taught the people and said:

3 "Those people who know they have great spiritual needs are happy. The kingdom of heaven belongs to them. 4 Those who are sad now are happy. God will comfort them. 5 Those who are humble are happy. The earth will belong to them. 6 Those who want to do right more than anything else are happy. God will fully satisfy them.

7 Those who give mercy to others are happy. Mercy will be given to them. 8 Those who are pure in their thinking are happy. They will be with God. 9 Those who work to bring peace are happy. God will call them his sons. 10 Those who are treated badly for doing good are happy. The kingdom of heaven belongs to them.

11 "People will say bad things about you and hurt you. They will lie and say all kinds of evil things about you because you follow me. But when they do these things to you, you are happy. 12 Rejoice and be glad. You have a great reward waiting for you in heaven. People did the same evil things to the prophets[d] who lived before you.

You Are like Salt and Light

13 "You are the salt of the earth. But if the salt loses its salty taste, it cannot be made salty again. It is good for nothing. It must be thrown out for people to walk on. 14 "You are the light that gives light to the world. A city that is built on a hill can-

not be hidden. 15 And people don't hide a light under a bowl. They put the light on a

lampstand. Then the light shines for all the people in the house.

16 "In the same way, you should be a light for other people. Live so that they will see the good things you do. Live so that they will praise your Father in heaven.

The Importance of the Law

17 "Don't think that I have come to destroy the law of Moses or the teaching of the prophets.[d] I have not come to destroy their teachings but to do what they said. 18 I tell you the truth. Nothing will disappear from the law until heaven and earth are gone. The law will not lose even the smallest letter or the smallest part of a letter until all has happened. 19 Whoever refuses to obey any command and teaches other people not to obey that command will be the least important in the kingdom of heaven. But whoever obeys the law and teaches other people to obey the law will be great in the kingdom of heaven. 20 I tell you that you must do better than the teachers of the law and the Pharisees.[d] If you are not better than they are, you will not enter the kingdom of heaven.

Jesus Teaches About Anger

21 "You have heard that it was said to our people long ago, 'You must not murder anyone.'[n] Anyone who murders another will be judged.' 22 But I tell you, if you are angry with your brother,[n] you will be judged. And if you say bad things to your brother, you will be judged by the Jewish council. And if you call your brother a fool, then you will be in danger of the fire of hell.
23 "So when you offer your gift to God at the altar, and you remember that your brother has something against you, 24 leave your gift there at the altar. Go and make peace with him. Then come and offer your gift.
25 "If your enemy is taking you to court, become friends with him quickly. You should do that before you go to court. If you don't become his friend, he might turn you over to the judge. And the judge might give you to a guard to put you in jail. 26 I tell you that you will not leave that jail until you have paid everything you owe.

Jesus Teaches About Sexual Sin

27 "You have heard that it was said, 'You must not be guilty of adultery.'[n] 28 But I tell you that if anyone looks at a woman and wants to sin sexually with her, then he has already done that sin with the woman in his mind. 29 If your right eye causes you to sin, then take it out and throw it away. It is better to lose one part of your body than to have your whole body thrown into hell. 30 If your right hand causes you to sin, then cut it off and throw it away. It is better to lose one part of your body than for your whole body to go into hell.

Jesus Teaches About Divorce

31 "It was also said, 'Anyone who divorces his wife must give her a written divorce paper.'[n] 32 But I tell you that anyone who divorces his wife is causing his wife to be guilty of adultery.[d] The only reason for a man to divorce his wife is if she has sexual relations with another man. And anyone who marries that divorced woman is guilty of adultery.

5:21 You . . . anyone. Quotation from Exodus 20:13; Deuteronomy 5:17.
5:22 brother Some Greek copies continue, "without a reason."
5:27 'You . . . adultery.' Quotation from Exodus 20:14; Deuteronomy 5:18.
5:31 'Anyone . . . divorce paper.' Quotation from Deuteronomy 24:1.

11

Make Promises Carefully

33 "You have heard that it was said to our people long ago, 'When you make a promise, don't break your promise. Keep the promises that you make to the Lord.'ⁿ
34 But I tell you, never make an oath. Don't make an oath using the name of heaven, because heaven is God's throne. 35 Don't make an oath using the name of the earth, because the earth belongs to God. Don't make an oath using the name of Jerusalem, because that is the city of the great King. 36 And don't even say that your own head is proof that you will keep your oath. You cannot make one hair on your head become white or black.
37 Say only 'yes' if you mean 'yes,' and say only 'no' if you mean 'no.' If you must say more than 'yes' or 'no,' it is from the Evil One.

Don't Fight Back

38 "You have heard that it was said, 'An eye for an eye, and a tooth for a tooth.'ⁿ
39 But I tell you, don't stand up against an evil person. If someone slaps you on the right cheek, then turn and let him slap the other cheek too. 40 If someone wants to sue you in court and take your shirt, then let him have your coat too. 41 If a soldier forces you to go with him one mile, then go with him two miles. 42 If a person asks you for something, then give it to him. Don't refuse to give to a person who wants to borrow from you.

Love All People

43 "You have heard that it was said, 'Love your neighborⁿ and hate your enemies.' 44 But I tell you, love your enemies. Pray for those who hurt you.ⁿ 45 If you do this, then you will be true sons of your Father in heaven. Your Father causes the sun to rise on good people and on bad people. Your Father sends rain to those who do good and to those who do wrong. 46 If you love only the people who love you, then you will get no reward. Even the tax collectors do that. 47 And if you are nice only to your friends, then you are no better than other people. Even people without God are nice to their friends. 48 So you must be perfect, just as your Father in heaven is perfect.

Chapter 6

Jesus Teaches About Giving

1 "Be careful! When you do good things, don't do them in front of people to be seen by them. If you do that, then you will have no reward from your Father in heaven.
2 "When you give to the poor, don't be like the hypocrites.ᵈ They blow trumpets before they give so that people will see them. They do that in the synagoguesᵈ and on the streets. They want other people to honor them. I tell you the truth. Those hypocrites already have their full reward. 3 So when you give to the poor, give very secretly. Don't let anyone know what you are doing. 4 Your giving should be done in secret. Your Father can see what is done in secret, and he will reward you.

Jesus Teaches About Prayer

5 "When you pray, don't be like the hypocrites.ᵈ They love to stand in the synagoguesᵈ and on the street corners and pray loudly. They want people to see them pray. I tell you the truth. They already have their full reward. 6 When you pray, you should go into your room and close the door. Then pray to your Father who cannot be seen. Your Father can see what is done in secret, and he will reward you.
7 "And when you pray, don't be like those people who don't know God. They continue saying things that mean nothing. They think that God will hear them because of the many things they say. 8 Don't be like them. Your Father knows the things you need before you ask him. 9 So when you pray, you should pray like this:

5:33 'When . . . Lord.' Quotation from Leviticus 19:12; Numbers 30:2; Deuteronomy 23:21. 5:38 'An eye . . . tooth.' Quotation from Exodus 21:24; Leviticus 24:20; Deuteronomy 19:21. 5:43 Love your neighbor Quotation from Leviticus 19:18. 5:44 you Some Greek copies continue, "Bless those who curse you, do good to those who hate you." Compare Luke 6:28.

'Our Father in heaven, we pray that your name will always be kept holy. 10 We pray that your kingdom will come. We pray that what you want will be done, here on earth as it is in heaven. 11 Give us the food we need for each day. 12 Forgive the sins we have done, just as we have forgiven those who did wrong to us.

13 Do not cause us to be tested;but save us from the Evil One.' [The kingdom, the power, and the glory are yours forever. Amen.]" 14 Yes, if you forgive others for the things they do wrong, then your Father in heaven will also forgive you for the things you do wrong.

15 But if you don't forgive the wrongs of others, then your Father in heaven will not forgive the wrong things you do.

Jesus Teaches About Worship

16 "When you give up eating," don't put on a sad face like the hypocrites.[d] They make their faces look strange to show people that they are giving up eating. I tell you the truth, those hypocrites already have their full reward. 17 So when you give up eating, comb your hair and wash your face. 18 Then people will not know that you are giving up eating. But your Father, whom you cannot see, will see you. Your Father sees what is done in secret, and he will reward you.

God Is More Important than Money

19 "Don't store treasures for yourselves here on earth. Moths and rust will destroy treasures here on earth. And thieves can break into your house and steal the things you have. 20 So store your treasure in heaven. The treasures in heaven cannot be destroyed by moths or rust. And thieves cannot break in and steal that treasure. 21 Your heart will be where your treasure is.
22 "The eye is a light for the body. If your eyes are good, then your whole body will be full of light. 23 But if your eyes are evil, then your whole body will be full of darkness. And if the only light you have is really darkness, then you have the worst darkness.
24 "No one can be a slave to two masters. He will hate one master and love the other. Or he will follow one master and refuse to follow the other. So you cannot serve God and money at the same time.

Don't Worry

25 "So I tell you, don't worry about the food you need to live. And don't worry about the clothes you need for your body. Life is more important than food. And the body is more important than clothes.

6:13 The . . . Amen. Some Greek copies do not contain the bracketed text.
6:16 give up eating This is called "fasting." The people would give up eating for a special time of prayer and worship to God. It was also done to show sadness.

26 "Look at the birds in the air. They don't plant or harvest or store food in barns. But your heavenly Father feeds the birds.

And you know that you are worth much more than the birds. 27 You cannot add any time to your life by worrying about it.
28 "And why do you worry about clothes? Look at the flowers in the field. See how they grow. They don't work or make clothes for themselves.

29 But I tell you that even Solomon with his riches was not dressed as beautifully as one of these flowers.

30 God clothes the grass in the field like that. The grass is living today, but tomorrow it is thrown into the fire to be burned. So you can be even more sure that God will clothe you. Don't have so little faith!
31 Don't worry and say, 'What will we eat?' or 'What will we drink?' or 'What will we wear?'
32 All the people who don't know God keep trying to get these things. And your Father in heaven knows that you

need them. 33 The thing you should want most is God's kingdom and doing what God wants. Then all these other things you need will be given

to you. 34 So don't worry about tomorrow. Each day has enough trouble of its own. Tomorrow will have its own worries.

Chapter 7

Be Careful About Judging Others

1 "Don't judge other people, and you will not be judged.
2 You will be judged in the same way that you judge others. And the forgiveness you give to others will be given to you.
3 "Why do you notice the little piece of dust that is in your brother's eye, but you don't notice the big piece of wood that is in your own eye? 4 Why do you say to your brother, 'Let me take that little piece

of dust out of your eye'? Look at yourself first! You still have that big piece of wood in your own eye. 5 You are a hypocrite!d First, take the wood out of your own eye. Then you will see clearly enough to take the dust out of your brother's eye.
6 "Don't give holy things to dogs. Don't throw your pearls before pigs. Pigs will only trample on them. And the dogs will only turn to attack you.

Ask God for What You Need

7 "Continue to ask, and God will give to you. Continue to search, and you will find. Continue to knock, and the door will open for you. 8 Yes, everyone who continues asking will receive. He who continues searching will find. And he who continues knocking will have the door opened for him.
9 "What would you do if your son asks for bread? Which of you would give him a stone? 10 Or if your son asks for a fish, would you give him a snake? 11 Even though you are bad, you know how to give good gifts to your children. So surely your heavenly Father will give good things to those who ask him.

People Know You by Your Actions

15 "Be careful of false prophets.[d] They come to you and look gentle like sheep. But they are really dangerous like wolves. 16 You will know these people because of the things they do. Good things don't come from bad people, just as grapes don't come from thornbushes. And figs don't come from thorny weeds. 17 In the same way, every good tree produces good fruit. And bad trees produce bad fruit. 18 A good tree cannot produce bad fruit. And a bad tree cannot produce good fruit. 19 Every tree that does not produce good fruit is cut down and thrown into the fire. 20 You will know these false prophets by what they produce.

21 "Not everyone who says 'You are my Lord' will enter the kingdom of heaven. The only people who will enter the kingdom of heaven are those who do the things that my Father in heaven wants. 22 On the last day many people will say to me, 'You are our Lord! We spoke for you. And through you we forced out demons[d] and did many miracles.'[d] 23 Then I will tell them clearly, 'Get away from me, you who do evil. I never knew you.'

The Most Important Rule

12 "Do for other people the same things you want them to do for you. This is the meaning of the law of Moses and the teaching of the prophets.[d]

The Way to Heaven Is Hard

13 "Enter through the narrow gate. The road that leads to hell is a very easy road. And the gate to hell is very wide. Many people enter through that gate. 14 But the gate that opens the way to true life is very small. And the road to true life is very hard. Only a few people find that road.

Two Kinds of People

24 "Everyone who hears these things I say and obeys them is like a wise man. The wise man built his house on rock. 25 It rained hard and the water rose. The winds blew and hit that house. But the house did not fall, because the house was built on rock. 26 But the person who hears the things I teach and does not obey them is like a foolish man. The foolish man built his house on sand. 27 It rained hard, the water rose, and the winds blew and hit that house. And the house fell with a big crash."

28 When Jesus finished saying these things, the people were amazed at his teaching. 29 Jesus did not teach like their teachers of the law. He taught like a person who had authority.

chapter

8

Jesus Heals a Sick Man

1 When Jesus came down from the hill, great crowds followed him. 2 Then a man sick with a harmful skin disease came to Jesus. The man bowed down before him and said,

"Lord, you have the power to heal me if you want."

Matthew 8:3-9

3 Jesus touched the man and said,

"I want to heal you. Be healed!"

And immediately the man was healed from his skin disease.

4 Then Jesus said to him,

"Don't tell anyone about what happened. But go and show yourself to the priest." And offer the gift that Moses commanded[n] for people who are made well. This will show people that you are healed."

Jesus Heals a Soldier's Servant

5 Jesus went to the city of Capernaum. When he entered the city, an army officer came to Jesus and begged for help. 6 The officer said,

"Lord, my servant is at home in bed. He can't move his body and is in much pain."

7 Jesus said to the officer,

"I will go and heal him."

8 The officer answered,

"Lord, I am not good enough for you to come into my house. All you need to do is command that my servant be healed, and he will be healed. 9 I myself am a man under the authority of other men. And I have soldiers under my command. I tell one soldier, 'Go,' and he goes. I tell another soldier, 'Come,' and he comes. I say to my servant, 'Do this,' and my servant obeys me."

8:4 show . . . priest The law of Moses said a priest must say when a Jew who had a harmful skin disease was well.
8:4 Moses commanded Read about this in Leviticus 14:1-32.

10 When Jesus heard this, he was amazed. He said to those who were with him,

"I tell you the truth. This man has more faith than any other person I have found, even in Israel. 11 Many people will come from the east and from the west. They will sit and eat with Abraham, Isaac, and Jacob in the kingdom of heaven. 12 And those people who should have the kingdom will be thrown outside into the darkness. In that place people will cry and grind their teeth with pain."

13 Then Jesus said to the officer,

"Go home. Your servant will be healed just as you believed he would."

And at that same time his servant was healed.

Jesus Heals Many People

14 Jesus went to Peter's house. There Jesus saw that Peter's mother-in-law was in bed with a high fever.

15 Jesus touched her hand, and the fever left her. Then she stood up and began to serve Jesus.
16 That evening people brought to Jesus many who had demons.[d] Jesus spoke and the demons left them. Jesus healed all the sick.

17 He did these things to make come true what Isaiah the prophet[d] said:

"He took our suffering on him. And he felt our pain for us."
Isaiah 53:4

People Want to Follow Jesus

18 When Jesus saw the crowd around him, he told his followers to go to the other side of the lake. 19 Then a teacher of the law came to Jesus and said,

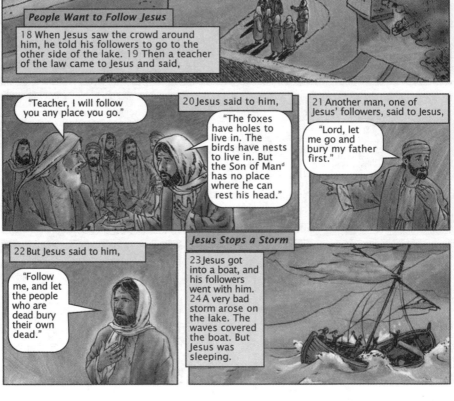

"Teacher, I will follow you any place you go."

20 Jesus said to him,

"The foxes have holes to live in. The birds have nests to live in. But the Son of Man[d] has no place where he can rest his head."

21 Another man, one of Jesus' followers, said to Jesus,

"Lord, let me go and bury my father first."

22 But Jesus said to him,

"Follow me, and let the people who are dead bury their own dead."

Jesus Stops a Storm

23 Jesus got into a boat, and his followers went with him. 24 A very bad storm arose on the lake. The waves covered the boat. But Jesus was sleeping.

25 The followers went to Jesus and woke him. They said,

"Lord, save us! We will drown!"

26 Jesus answered,

"Why are you afraid? You don't have enough faith."

Then Jesus got up and gave a command to the wind and the sea.

The wind stopped, and the sea became very calm.

27 The men were amazed. They said,

"What kind of man is this? Even the wind and the sea obey him!"

Jesus Heals Two Men with Demons

28 Jesus arrived at the other side of the lake in the country of the Gadarene[n] people. There, two men came to Jesus. They had demons[d] in them. These men lived in the burial caves. They were so dangerous that people could not use the road by those caves. 29 The two men came to Jesus and shouted,

"What do you want with us, Son of God? Did you come here to punish us before the right time?"

30 Near that place there was a large herd of pigs feeding.

31 The demons begged Jesus,

"If you make us leave these men, please send us into that herd of pigs."

32 Jesus said to them,

"Go!"

So the demons left the men and went into the pigs. Then the whole herd of pigs ran down the hill into the lake and were drowned.

8:28 **Gadarene** From Gadara, an area southeast of Lake Galilee. The exact location is uncertain and some Greek copies read "Gergesene"; others read "Gerasene."

33 The men who were caring for the pigs ran away and went into town. They told about all of this and what had happened to the men who had demons. 34 Then the whole town went out to see Jesus. When they saw him, they begged him to leave their area.

Chapter

9

Jesus Heals a Paralyzed Man

1 Jesus got into a boat and went back across the lake to his own town.

2 Some people brought to Jesus a man who was paralyzed. The man was lying on his mat. Jesus saw that these people had great faith, so he said to the paralyzed man,

"Be happy, young man. Your sins are forgiven."

3 Some of the teachers of the law heard this. They said to themselves,

"This man speaks as if he were God—that is blasphemy!"[n]

4 Jesus knew what they were thinking. So he said,

"Why are you thinking evil thoughts? 5 Which is easier: to tell this paralyzed man, 'Your sins are forgiven,' or to tell him, 'Stand up and walk'? 6 But I will prove to you that the Son of Man[d] has power on earth to forgive sins."

Then Jesus said to the paralyzed man,

"Stand up. Take your mat and go home."

7 And the man stood up and went home. 8 The people saw this and were amazed. They praised God for giving power like this to men.

9:3 blasphemy Saying things against God.

Jesus Chooses Matthew

9 When Jesus was leaving, he saw a man named Matthew. Matthew was sitting in the tax office. Jesus said to him,

"Follow me."

And Matthew stood up and followed Jesus.
10 Jesus had dinner at Matthew's house. Many tax collectors and "sinners" came and ate with Jesus and his followers.
11 The Pharisees[d] saw this and asked Jesus' followers,

"Why does your teacher eat with tax collectors and 'sinners'?"

12 Jesus heard the Pharisees ask this. So he said,

"Healthy people don't need a doctor. Only the sick need a doctor.

13 Go and learn what this means: 'I want faithful love more than I want animal sacrifices.'[n] I did not come to invite good people. I came to invite sinners."

Jesus Is Not like Other Jews

14 Then the followers of John[n] came to Jesus. They said to Jesus,

"We and the Pharisees[d] often give up eating.[n] But your followers don't. Why?"

15 Jesus answered,

"The friends of the bridegroom are not sad while he is with them. But the time will come when the bridegroom will leave them. Then his friends are sad, and they will give up eating.
16 "When someone sews a patch over a hole in an old coat, he never uses a piece of cloth that is not yet shrunk.

If he does, the patch will shrink and pull away from the coat. Then the hole will be worse. 17 Also, people never pour new wine into

old leather bags for holding wine. If they do, the old bags will break. The wine will spill, and the wine bags will be ruined. But people always

pour new wine into new wine bags. Then the wine and the wine bags will continue to be good."

9:13 'I want . . . sacrifices.' Quotation from Hosea 6:6. 9:14 John John the Baptist, who preached to people about Christ's coming (Matthew 3, Luke 3). 9:14 give up eating This is called "fasting." The people would give up eating for a special time of prayer and worship to God. It was also done to show sadness.

Matthew 9:18-27

Jesus Gives Life to a Dead Girl and Heals a Sick Woman

18 While Jesus was saying these things, a ruler of the synagogue[d] came to him. The ruler bowed down before Jesus and said,

"My daughter has just died. But come and touch her with your hand, and she will live again."

19 So Jesus stood up and went with the ruler. Jesus' followers went too. 20 Then a woman who had been bleeding for 12 years came behind Jesus and touched the edge of his coat.

21 She was thinking,

"If I can touch his coat, then I will be healed."

22 Jesus turned and saw the woman. He said,

"Be happy, dear woman. You are made well because you believed."

And the woman was healed at once.

23 Jesus continued along with the ruler and went into the ruler's house. Jesus saw people there who play music for funerals. And he saw many people there crying. 24 Jesus said,

"Go away. The girl is not dead. She is only asleep."

But the people laughed at Jesus.

Jesus Heals More People

25 After the crowd had been put outside, Jesus went into the girl's room. He took her hand,

and she stood up.

26 The news about this spread all around the area.

27 When Jesus was leaving there, two blind men followed him. They cried out,

"Show kindness to us, Son of David!"[d]

28 Jesus went inside, and the blind men went with him. He asked the men,

"Do you believe that I can make you see again?"

They answered, "Yes, Lord."

29 Then Jesus touched their eyes and said,

"You believe that I can make you see again. So this will happen."

30 Then the men were able to see.

But Jesus warned them very strongly, saying,

"Don't tell anyone about this."

31 But the blind men left and spread the news about Jesus all around that area.

32 When the two men were leaving, some people brought another man to Jesus. This man could not talk because he had a demon[d] in him.

33 Jesus forced the demon to leave the man. Then the man who couldn't talk was able to speak. The crowd was amazed and said,

"We have never seen anything like this in Israel."

34 But the Pharisees[d] said,

"The leader of demons is the one that gives him power to force demons out."

35 Jesus traveled through all the towns and villages. He taught in their synagogues[d] and told people the Good News[d] about the kingdom. And he healed all kinds of diseases and sicknesses. 36 He saw the crowds of people and felt sorry for them because they were worried and helpless. They were like sheep without a shepherd.

23

37 Jesus said to his followers,

"There are many people to harvest, but there are only a few workers to help harvest them. 38 God owns the harvest. Pray to him that he will send more workers to help gather his harvest."[n]

Chapter
10

Jesus Sends Out His Apostles

1 Jesus called his 12 followers together. He gave them power to drive out evil spirits and to heal every kind of disease and sickness.

2 These are the names of the 12 apostles:[d]

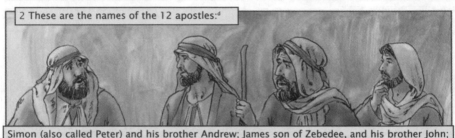

Simon (also called Peter) and his brother Andrew; James son of Zebedee, and his brother John;

3 Philip and Bartholomew; Thomas and Matthew, the tax collector;

James son of Alphaeus, and Thaddaeus; 4 Simon the Zealot[d] and Judas Iscariot. Judas is the one who turned against Jesus.

9:37-38 "There are . . . harvest." As a farmer sends workers to harvest the grain, Jesus sends his followers to bring people to God.

5 These 12 men he sent out with the following order:

"Don't go to the non-Jewish people. And don't go into any town where the Samaritans[d] live. 6 But go to the people of Israel. They are like sheep that are lost. 7 When you go, preach this: 'The kingdom of heaven is coming soon.' 8 Heal the sick. Give dead people life again. Heal those who have harmful skin diseases. Force demons[d] to leave people. I give you these powers freely. So help other people freely. 9 Don't carry any money with you—gold or silver or copper. 10 Don't carry a bag. Take for your trip only the clothes and sandals you are wearing. Don't take a walking stick. A worker should be given the things he needs.

11 "When you enter a city or town, find some worthy person there and stay in his home until you leave. 12 When you enter that home, say, 'Peace be with you.' 13 If the people there welcome you, let your peace stay there. But if they don't welcome you, take back the peace you wished for them. 14 And if a home or town refuses to welcome you or listen to you, then leave that place. Shake its dust off your feet." 15 I tell you the truth. On the Judgment Day it will be worse for that town than for the towns of Sodom and Gomorrah."

Jesus Warns His Apostles

16 "Listen! I am sending you out, and you will be like sheep among wolves. So be as smart as snakes. But also be like doves and do nothing wrong. 17 Be careful of people. They will arrest you and take you to court. They will whip you in their synagogues.[d] 18 Because of me you will be taken to stand before governors and kings. You will tell them and the non-Jewish people about me.

10:14 Shake . . . feet. A warning. It showed that they were finished talking to these people. **10:15 Sodom and Gomorrah** Two cities that God destroyed because the people were so evil.

19 "When you are arrested, don't worry about what to say or how you should say it. At that time you will be given the things to say. 20 It will not really be you speaking. The Spirit of your Father will be speaking through you.

21 "Brothers will turn against their own brothers and give them over to be killed. Fathers will turn against their own children and give them to be killed. Children will fight against their own parents and have them killed. 22 All people will hate you because you follow me. But the person who continues strong until the end will be saved. 23 When you are treated badly in one city, go to another city. I tell you the truth. You will not finish going through all the cities of Israel before the Son of Man[d] comes.

24 "A student is not better than his teacher. A servant is not better than his master. 25 A student should be satisfied to become like his teacher. A servant should be satisfied to become like his master. If the head of the family is called Beelzebul,[d] then the other members of the family will be called worse names!

Fear God, Not People

26 "So don't be afraid of those people. Everything that is hidden will be shown. Everything that is secret will be made known. 27 I tell you these things in the dark, but I want you to tell them in the light. I speak these things only to you, but you should tell them to everyone. 28 Don't be afraid of people. They can only kill the body. They cannot kill the soul. The only one you should fear is the One who can destroy the body and the soul in hell. 29 When birds are sold, two small birds cost only a penny. But not even one of the little birds can die without your Father's knowing it. 30 God even knows how many hairs are on your head. 31 So don't be afraid. You are worth much more than many birds.

Tell People About Your Faith

32 "If anyone stands before other people and says he believes in me, then I will say that he belongs to me. I will say this before my Father in heaven. 33 But if anyone stands before people and says he does not believe in me, then I will say that he does not belong to me. I will say this before my Father in heaven.

34 "Don't think that I have come to bring peace to the earth. I did not come to bring peace, but a sword. 35 I have come to make this happen:

'A son will be against his father, a daughter will be against her mother, a daughter-in-law will be against her mother-in-law.

36 A person's enemies will be members of his own family.'

Micah 7:6

37 "Whoever loves his father or mother more than he loves me is not worthy to be my follower. Whoever loves his son or daughter more than he loves me is not worthy to be my follower. 38 Whoever is not willing to die on a cross and follow me is not worthy of me. 39 Whoever tries to hold on to his life will give up true life. Whoever gives up his life for me will hold on to true life. 40 Whoever accepts you also accepts me. And whoever accepts me also accepts the One who sent me. 41 Whoever meets a prophet[d] and accepts him will receive the reward of a prophet. And whoever accepts a good man because that man is good will receive the reward of a good man. 42 Whoever helps one of these little ones because they are my followers will truly get his reward. He will get his reward even if he only gave my follower a cup of cold water."

Chapter 11

Jesus and John the Baptist

1 Jesus finished telling these things to his 12 followers. Then he left there and went to the towns in Galilee to teach and preach.

2 John the Baptist[d] was in prison, but he heard about the things the Christ was doing. So John sent some of his followers to Jesus. 3 They asked Jesus,

"Are you the man who John said was coming, or should we wait for another one?"

4 Jesus answered,

"Go back to John and tell him about the things you hear and see: 5 The blind can see. The crippled can walk. People with harmful skin diseases are healed. The deaf can hear. The dead are raised to life. And the Good News[d] is told to the poor. 6 The person who does not lose faith because of me is blessed."

7 As John's followers were leaving, Jesus began talking to the people about John. Jesus said,

"What did you go out to the desert to see? A reed[n] blown by the wind? No. 8 Really, what did you go out to see? A man dressed in fine clothes? No. Those people who wear fine clothes live in kings' palaces.

11:7 reed It means that John was not weak like grass blown by the wind.

9 "So what did you go out to see? A prophet?[d] Yes, and I tell you, John is more than a prophet. 10 This was written about John in the Scriptures: [d]

'I will send my messenger ahead of you. He will prepare the way for you.'
Malachi 3:1

11 I tell you the truth: John the Baptist is greater than any other man who has ever lived. But even the least important person in the kingdom of heaven is greater than John. 12 Since the time John the Baptist came until now, the kingdom of heaven has been going forward in strength. People using force have been trying to take the kingdom. 13 All the prophets and the law of Moses spoke until the time John came. They told about the things that would happen. 14 And if you will believe the things the law and the prophets said, then you will believe that John is Elijah. The law and the prophets said he would come. 15 Let those with ears use them and listen!

16 "What can I say about the people who live today? What are they like? They are like children sitting in the marketplace. One group calls to the other, 17 'We played music for you, but you did not dance; we sang a sad song, but you did not cry.' 18 John came, and he did not eat like other people or drink wine. And people say, 'He has a demon.'[d] 19 The Son of Man[d] came, eating and drinking wine, and people say, 'Look at him! He eats too much and drinks too much. He is a friend of tax collectors and "sinners." ' But wisdom is proved to be right by the things it does."

Jesus Warns Unbelievers

20 Then Jesus criticized the cities where he did most of his miracles.[d] He criticized them because the people there did not change their lives and stop sinning.

21 Jesus said,

"How terrible for you, Korazin! How terrible for you, Bethsaida! I did many miracles in you. If those same miracles had happened in Tyre and Sidon,[n] then the people there would have changed their lives a long time ago. They would have worn rough cloth and put ashes on themselves to show that they had changed. 22 But I tell you, on the Judgment Day it will be worse for you than for Tyre and Sidon. 23 And you, Capernaum,[n] will you be lifted up to heaven? No. You will be thrown down to the depths. I did many miracles in you. If those same miracles had happened in Sodom,[n] its people would have stopped sinning, and it would still be a city today. 24 But I tell you it will be worse for you on the Judgment Day than for Sodom."

11:21 Tyre and Sidon Towns where wicked people lived.
11:21-23 Korazin . . . Bethsaida . . . Capernaum Towns by Lake Galilee where Jesus preached to the people. **11:23 Sodom** City that God destroyed because the people were so evil.

Jesus Offers Rest to People

25 Then Jesus said,

"I thank you, Father, Lord of heaven and earth. I praise you because you have hidden these things from the people who are wise and smart. But you have shown them to those who are like little children.

26 Yes, Father, this is what you really wanted.

27 "My Father has given me all things. No one knows the Son—only the Father knows the Son. And no one knows the Father—only the Son knows the Father. And the only people who will know about the Father are those whom the Son chooses to tell.
28 "Come to me, all of you who are tired and have heavy loads. I will give you rest.
29 Accept my work and learn from me. I am gentle and humble in spirit. And you will find rest for your souls. 30 The work that I ask you to accept is easy. The load I give you to carry is not heavy."

Chapter

12

Jesus Is Lord of the Sabbath

1 About that same time, Jesus was walking through some fields of grain on a Sabbath[d] day. His followers were with him, and they were hungry. So they began to pick the grain and eat it.

2 The Pharisees[d] saw this, and they said to Jesus,

"Look! Your followers are doing something that is against the Jewish law to do on the Sabbath day."

3 Jesus answered,

"Have you not read what David did when he and the people with him were hungry? 4 David went into God's house. He and those with him ate the bread that was made holy for God. It was against the law for them to eat that bread. Only the priests were allowed to eat it.

Matthew 12:5-14

5 "And have you not read in the law of Moses that on every Sabbath day the priests in the Temple[d] break this law about the Sabbath day? But the priests are not wrong for doing that. 6 I tell you that there is something here that is greater than the Temple. 7 The Scripture[d] says, 'I want faithful love more than I want animal sacrifices.'[n] You don't really know what those words mean. If you understood them, you would not judge those who have done nothing wrong.
8 "The Son of Man[d] is Lord of the Sabbath day."

Jesus Heals a Man's Crippled Hand

9 Jesus left there and went into their synagogue.[d]

10 In the synagogue, there was a man with a crippled hand. Some Jews there were looking for a reason to accuse Jesus of doing wrong. So they asked him,

"Is it right to heal on the Sabbath[d] day?"[n]

11 Jesus answered,

"If any of you has a sheep, and it falls into a ditch on the Sabbath day, then you will take the sheep and help it out of the ditch. 12 Surely a man is more important than a sheep. So the law of Moses allows people to do good things on the Sabbath day."

13 Then Jesus said to the man with the crippled hand,

"Let me see your hand."

The man put his hand out,

and the hand became well again, the same as the other hand.

14 But the Pharisees[d] left and made plans to kill Jesus.

12:7 'I . . . sacrifices.' Quotation from Hosea 6:6.
12:10 "Is it right . . . day?" It was against Jewish law to work on the Sabbath day.

30

Jesus Is God's Chosen Servant

15 Jesus knew what the Pharisees[d] were doing, so he left that place. Many people followed him, and he healed all who were sick. 16 But Jesus warned the people not to tell who he was. 17 He did these things to make come true what Isaiah the prophet[d] had said:

18 "Here is my servant whom I have chosen. I love him, and I am pleased with him. I will put my Spirit[d] in him. Then he will tell how I will judge all people fairly. 19 He will not argue or shout. No one will hear his voice in the streets. 20 He will not break a crushed blade of grass. He will not put out even a weak flame. He will continue until he makes fair judgment win the victory. 21 In him will the nations find hope."

Isaiah 42:1-4

Jesus' Power Is from God

22 Then some people brought a man to Jesus. This man was blind and could not talk, because he had a demon.[d] Jesus healed the man, and the man could talk and see.

23 All the people were amazed. They said,

"Perhaps this man is the Son of David!"[d]

24 The Pharisees[d] heard the people saying this. The Pharisees said,

"Jesus uses the power of Beelzebul[d] to force demons out of people. Beelzebul is the ruler of demons."

25 Jesus knew what the Pharisees were thinking. So he said to them,

"Every kingdom that is fighting against itself will be destroyed. And every city that is divided will fall. And every family that is divided cannot succeed. 26 So if Satan forces out his own demons, then Satan is divided, and his kingdom will not continue.

27 "You say that I use the power of Satan when I force out demons. If that is true, then what power do your people use when they force out demons? So your own people prove that you are wrong. 28 But if I use the power of God's Spirit[d] to force out demons, this shows that the kingdom of God has come to you. 29 "If anyone wants to enter a strong man's house and steal his things, first he must tie up the strong man. Then he can steal the things from the strong man's house. 30 "If anyone is not with me, then he is against me. He who does not work with me is working against me. 31 So I tell you, people can be forgiven for every sin they do. And people can be forgiven for every bad thing they say. But if anyone speaks against the Holy Spirit, then he will not be forgiven. 32 Anyone who says things against the Son of Man[d] can be forgiven. But anyone who says things against the Holy Spirit will not be forgiven. He will not be forgiven now or in the future.

People Know You by Your Words

33 "If you want good fruit, you must make the tree good. If your tree is not good, then it will have bad fruit. A tree is known by the kind of fruit it produces. 34 You snakes! You are evil people! How can you say anything good? The mouth speaks the things that are in the heart. 35 A good person has good things in his heart. And so he speaks the good things that come from his heart. But an evil person has evil in his heart. So he speaks the evil things that come from his heart. 36 And I tell you that people will have to explain about every careless thing they have said. This will happen on the Judgment Day. 37 The words you have said will be used to judge you. Some of your words will prove you right, but some of your words will prove you guilty."

The Leaders Ask for a Miracle

38 Then some of the Pharisees[d] and teachers of the law answered Jesus. They said,

"Teacher, we want to see you work a miracle[d] as a sign."

39 Jesus answered,

"Evil and sinful people are the ones who want to see a miracle for a sign. But no sign will be given to them. The only sign will be what happened to the prophet[d] Jonah. 40 Jonah was in the stomach of the big fish for three days and three nights. In the same way, the Son of Man[d] will be in the grave three days and three nights. 41 And on the Judgment Day the men from Nineveh[n] will stand up with you people who live today. They will show that you are guilty because when Jonah preached to them, they were sorry and changed their lives. And I tell you that someone greater than Jonah is here! 42 On the Judgment Day, the Queen of the South[n] will stand up with you people who live today. She will show that you are guilty because she came from far away to listen to Solomon's wise teaching. And I tell you that someone greater than Solomon is here!

People Today Are Full of Evil

43 "When an evil spirit comes out of a man, it travels through dry places looking for a place to rest. But it finds no place to rest. 44 So the spirit says, 'I will go back to the home I left.' When the spirit comes back to the man, the spirit finds the home still empty. The home is swept clean and made neat. 45 Then the evil spirit goes out and brings seven other spirits even more evil than it is. Then all the spirits go into the man and live there. And that man has even more trouble than he had before. It is the same way with the evil people who live today."

12:41 **Nineveh** The city where Jonah preached to warn the people. Read Jonah 3.
12:42 **Queen of the South** The Queen of Sheba. She traveled 1,000 miles to learn God's wisdom from Solomon. Read 1 Kings 10:1-13.

33

Jesus' True Family

46 While Jesus was talking to the people, his mother and brothers stood outside. They wanted to talk to him. 47 Someone told Jesus,

"Your mother and brothers are waiting for you outside. They want to talk to you."ⁿ

48 He answered,

"Who is my mother? Who are my brothers?"

49 Then he pointed to his followers and said,

"See! These people are my mother and my brothers. 50 My true brothers and sisters and mother are those who do the things that my Father in heaven wants."

Chapter

13

A Story About Planting Seed

1 That same day Jesus went out of the house and sat by the lake. 2 Large crowds gathered around him. So Jesus got into a boat and sat, while the people stayed on the shore. 3 Then Jesus used stories to teach them many things. He said:

"A farmer went out to plant his seed. 4 While he was planting, some seed fell by the road. The birds came and ate all that seed. 5 Some seed fell on rocky ground, where there wasn't enough dirt. That seed grew very fast, because the ground was not deep. 6 But when the sun rose, the plants dried up because they did not have deep roots.

12:47 Someone . . . you. Some Greek copies do not have verse 47.

7 "Some other seed fell among thorny weeds. The weeds grew and choked the good plants. 8 Some other seed fell on good ground where it grew and became grain. Some plants made 100 times more grain. Other plants made 60 times more grain, and some made 30 times more grain.

9 Let those with ears use them and listen!"

Why Jesus Used Stories to Teach

10 The followers came to Jesus and asked,

"Why do you use stories to teach the people?"

11 Jesus answered,

"Only you can know the secret truths about the kingdom of heaven. Other people cannot know these secret truths. 12 The person who has something will be given more. And he will have all he needs. But the person who does not have much, even what he has will be taken from him. 13 This is why I use stories to teach the people: They see, but they don't really see. They hear, but they don't really understand. 14 So they show that the things Isaiah said about them are true:

'You will listen and listen, but you will not understand. You will look and look, but you will not learn. 15 For these people have become stubborn. They do not hear with their ears. And they have closed their eyes. Otherwise they might really understand what they see with their eyes and hear with their ears. They might really understand in their minds. If they did this, they would come back to me and be forgiven.'

Isaiah 6:9,10

35

16 "But you are blessed. You understand the things you see with your eyes. And you understand the things you hear with your ears. 17 I tell you the truth. Many prophets[d] and good people wanted to see the things that you now see. But they did not see them. And many prophets and good people wanted to hear the things that you now hear. But they did not hear them.

Jesus Explains the Seed Story

18 "So listen to the meaning of that story about the farmer. 19 What is the seed that fell by the road? That seed is like the person who hears the teaching about the kingdom but does not understand it. The Evil One comes and takes away the things that were planted in that person's heart. 20 And what is the seed that fell on rocky ground? That seed is like the person who hears the teaching and quickly accepts it with joy. 21 But he does not let the teaching go deep into his life. He keeps it only a short time. When trouble or persecution comes because of the teaching he accepted, then he quickly gives up. 22 And what is the seed that fell among the thorny weeds? That seed is like the person who hears the teaching but lets worries about this life and love of money stop that teaching from growing. So the teaching does not produce fruit[n] in that person's life. 23 But what is the seed that fell on the good ground? That seed is like the person who hears the teaching and understands it. That person grows and produces fruit, sometimes 100 times more, sometimes 60 times more, and sometimes 30 times more."

A Story About Wheat and Weeds

24 Then Jesus told them another story. He said,

"The kingdom of heaven is like a man who planted good seed in his field. 25 That night, when everyone was asleep, his enemy came and planted weeds among the wheat. Then the enemy went away. 26 Later, the wheat grew and heads of grain grew on the wheat plants. But at the same time the weeds also grew. 27 Then the man's servants came to him and said,

'You planted good seed in your field. Where did the weeds come from?'

28 The man answered,

'An enemy planted weeds.'

The servants asked,

'Do you want us to pull up the weeds?'

29 The man answered,

'No, because when you pull up the weeds, you might also pull up the wheat.

30 Let the weeds and the wheat grow together until the harvest time. At harvest time I will tell the workers this: First gather the weeds and tie them together to be burned.

Then gather the wheat and bring it to my barn.' "

13:22 produce fruit To produce fruit means to have in your life the good things God wants.

Stories of Mustard Seed and Yeast

31 Then Jesus told another story:

"The kingdom of heaven is like a mustard seed. A man plants the seed in his field. 32 That seed is the smallest of all seeds.

But when it grows, it is one of the largest garden plants. It becomes a tree, big enough for the wild birds to come and make nests in its branches."

33 Then Jesus told another story:

"The kingdom of heaven is like yeast that a woman mixes into a big bowl of flour. The yeast makes all the dough rise."

34 Jesus used stories to tell all these things to the people. He always used stories to teach people. 35 This is as the prophet[d] said:

"I will speak using stories;
I will tell things that have been secret since the world was made."
Psalm 78.2

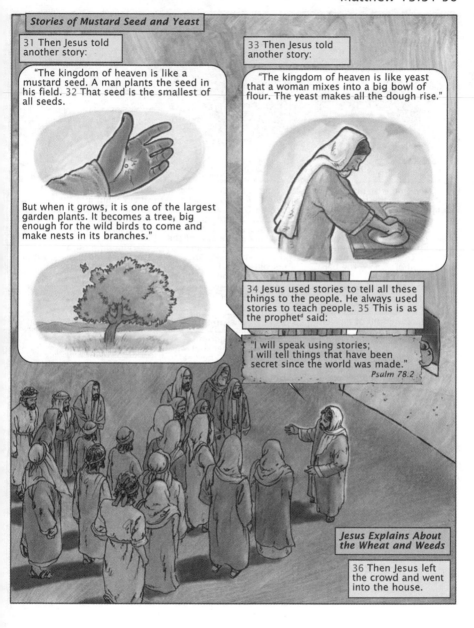

Jesus Explains About the Wheat and Weeds

36 Then Jesus left the crowd and went into the house.

His followers came to him and said,

"Explain to us the meaning of the story about the weeds in the field."

37 Jesus answered,

"The man who planted the good seed in the field is the Son of Man.[d] 38 The field is the world. And the good seed are all of God's children in the kingdom. The weeds are those people who belong to the Evil One. 39 And the enemy who planted the bad seed is the devil. The harvest time is the end of the age. And the workers who gather are God's angels. 40 "The weeds are pulled up and burned in the fire. It will be this way at the end of the age. 41 The Son of Man will send out his angels. They will gather out of his kingdom all who cause sin and all who do evil. 42 The angels will throw them into the blazing furnace. There the people will cry and grind their teeth with pain. 43 Then the good people will shine like the sun in the kingdom of their Father. Let those with ears use them and listen!

Stories of a Treasure and a Pearl

44 "The kingdom of heaven is like a treasure hidden in a field. One day a man found the treasure, and then he hid it in the field again. The man was very happy to find the treasure. He went and sold everything that he owned to buy that field.

45 "Also, the kingdom of heaven is like a man looking for fine pearls. 46 One day he found a very valuable pearl. The man went and sold everything he had to buy that pearl.

A Story of a Fishing Net

47 "Also, the kingdom of heaven is like a net that was put into the lake. The net caught many different kinds of fish.

48 When it was full, the fishermen pulled the net to the shore. They sat down and put all the good fish in baskets. Then they threw away the bad fish.

49 "It will be this way at the end of the age. The angels will come and separate the evil people from the good people. 50 The angels will throw the evil people into the blazing furnace. In that place the people will cry and grind their teeth with pain."

They answered,

"Yes, we understand."

51 Jesus asked his followers,

"Do you understand all these things?"

52 Then Jesus said to them,

"So every teacher of the law who has been taught about the kingdom of heaven is like the owner of a house. He has both new things and old things saved in his house. And he brings out both those new things and old things."

Jesus Goes to His Hometown

53 When Jesus finished teaching with these stories, he left there. 54 He went to the town where he grew up. He taught the people in the synagogue[d] and they were amazed. They said,

"Where did this man get this wisdom and this power to do miracles?[d] 55 He is only the son of the carpenter. And his mother is Mary. His brothers are James, Joseph, Simon and Judas. 56 And all his sisters are here with us. So where does this man get all these things?"

"A prophet[d] is honored everywhere except in his own town or in his home."

57 And the people refused to accept Jesus. But Jesus said to them,

58 The people there did not believe in Jesus. So Jesus did not do many miracles there.

Chapter
14

How John the Baptist Was Killed

1 At that time Herod, the ruler of Galilee, heard the reports about Jesus. 2 So Herod said to his servants,

"Jesus is really John the Baptist[d] He has risen from death. That is why he is able to do these miracles."[d]

3 Sometime before this, Herod had arrested John, tied him up, and put him into prison. Herod did this because of Herodias. Herodias was the wife of Philip, Herod's brother. 4 Herod arrested John because he told Herod:

"It is not right for you to have Herodias."

5 Herod wanted to kill John, but he was afraid of the people. They believed that John was a prophet.[d]

6 On Herod's birthday, the daughter of Herodias danced for Herod and his guests. Herod was very pleased with her, 7 so he promised he would give her anything she wanted.

8 Herodias told her daughter what to ask for. So she said to Herod,

"Give me the head of John the Baptist here on a platter."

9 King Herod was very sad. But he had promised to give her anything she wanted, and the people eating with him had heard his promise. So Herod ordered that what she asked for be done. 10 He sent men to the prison to cut off John's head. 11 And the men brought John's head on a platter and gave it to the girl. She took it to her mother, Herodias. 12 John's followers came and got his body and buried it. Then they went and told Jesus what happened.

More than 5,000 People Fed

15 Late that afternoon, his followers came to Jesus and said,

"No one lives in this place. And it is already late. Send the people away so they can go to the towns and buy food for themselves."

13 When Jesus heard what happened to John, Jesus left in a boat. He went to a lonely place by himself. But when the crowds heard about it, they followed him on foot from the towns. 14 When Jesus arrived, he saw a large crowd. He felt sorry for them and healed those who were sick.

16 Jesus answered,

"They don't need to go away. You give them some food to eat."

17 The followers answered,

"But we have only five loaves of bread and two fish."

18 Jesus said,

"Bring the bread and the fish to me."

19 Then he told the people to sit down on the grass. He took the five loaves of bread and the two fish. Then he looked to heaven and thanked God for the food. Jesus divided the loaves of bread. He gave them to his followers,

and they gave the bread to the people. 20 All the people ate and were satisfied. After they finished eating, the followers filled 12 baskets with the pieces of food that were not eaten. 21 There were about 5,000 men there who ate, as well as women and children.

Matthew 14:22-31

Jesus Walks on the Water

22 Then Jesus made his followers get into the boat. He told them to go ahead of him to the other side of the lake. Jesus stayed there to tell the people they could go home. 23 After he said good-bye to them, he went alone up into the hills to pray. It was late, and Jesus was there alone.

24 By this time, the boat was already far away on the lake. The boat was having trouble because of the waves, and the wind was blowing against it.

25 Between three and six o'clock in the morning, Jesus' followers were still in the boat. Jesus came to them. He was walking on the water.

26 When the followers saw him walking on the water, they were afraid. They said,

"It's a ghost!"

and cried out in fear.

27 But Jesus quickly spoke to them. He said,

"Have courage! It is I! Don't be afraid."

28 Peter said,

"Lord, if that is really you, then tell me to come to you on the water."

29 Jesus said,

"Come."

And Peter left the boat and walked on the water to Jesus. 30 But when Peter saw the wind and the waves, he became afraid and began to sink. He shouted,

"Lord, save me!"

31 Then Jesus reached out his hand and caught Peter. Jesus said,

"Your faith is small. Why did you doubt?"

32 After Peter and Jesus were in the boat, the wind became calm. 33 Then those who were in the boat worshiped Jesus and said,

"Truly you are the Son of God!"

34 After they crossed the lake, they came to the shore at Gennesaret. 35 The people there saw Jesus and knew who he was. So they told people all around there that Jesus had come. They brought all their sick to him. 36 They begged Jesus to let them just touch the edge of his coat to be healed. And all the sick people who touched it were healed.

chapter

15

Obey God's Law Not Men's

1 Then some Pharisees[d] and teachers of the law came to Jesus from Jerusalem. They asked him,

2 "Why do your followers not obey the rules given to us by the great people who lived before us? Your followers don't wash their hands before they eat!"

3 Jesus answered,

"And why do you refuse to obey God's command so that you can follow those rules you have? 4 God said, 'Honor your father and mother.'[n] And God also said, 'Anyone who says cruel things to his father or mother must be put to death.'[n] 5 But you say that a person can tell his father or mother, 'I have some-thing I could use to help you. But I will not use it for you. I will give it to God.' 6 You teach that person not to honor his father. You teach that it is not important to do what God said. You think that it is more important to follow the rules you have. 7 You are hypocrites![d] Isaiah was right when he spoke about you:

8 'These people show honor to me with words. But their hearts are far from me. 9 Their worship of me is worthless. The things they teach are nothing but human rules they have memorized.' "
Isaiah 29:13

15:4 'Honor . . . mother.' Quotation from Exodus 20:12; Deuteronomy 5:16.
15:4 'Anyone . . . death.' Quotation from Exodus 21:17.

10 Jesus called the crowd to him. He said,

"Listen and understand what I am saying. 11 It is not what a person puts into his mouth that makes him unclean[d] It is what comes out of his mouth that makes him unclean."

12 Then his followers came to Jesus and asked,

"Do you know that the Pharisees are angry because of what you said?"

13 Jesus answered,

"Every plant that my Father in heaven has not planted himself will be pulled up by the roots. 14 Stay away from the Pharisees. They are blind leaders.[n] And if a blind man leads another blind man, then both men will fall into a ditch."

15 Peter said,

"Explain the story to us."

16 Jesus said,

"You still have trouble understanding? 17 Surely you know that all the food that enters the mouth goes into the stomach. Then that food goes out of the body. 18 But what a person says with his mouth comes from the way he thinks. And these are the things that make him unclean.

19 Out of his mind come evil thoughts, murder, adultery,[d] sexual sins, stealing, lying, and saying bad things against other people. 20 These things make a person unclean. But eating with unwashed hands does not make him unclean."

Jesus Helps a Non-Jewish Woman

21 Jesus left that place and went to the area of Tyre and Sidon.

15:14 leaders Some Greek copies continue, "of blind people."

22 A Canaanite woman from that area came to Jesus. The woman cried out,

"Lord, Son of David,[d] please help me! My daughter has a demon,[d] and she is suffering very much."

23 But Jesus did not answer the woman. So the followers came to Jesus and begged him,

"Tell the woman to go away. She is following us and shouting."

24 Jesus answered,

"God sent me only to the lost sheep, the people of Israel."

25 Then the woman came to Jesus again. She bowed before him and said,

"Lord, help me!"

26 Jesus answered,

"It is not right to take the children's bread and give it to the dogs."

27 The woman said,

"Yes, Lord, but even the dogs eat the pieces of food that fall from their masters' table."

28 Then Jesus answered,

"Woman, you have great faith! I will do what you asked me to do."

And at that moment the woman's daughter was healed.

Jesus Heals Many People

29 Then Jesus left that place and went to the shore of Lake Galilee. He went up on a hill and sat there.
30 Great crowds came to Jesus. They brought their sick with them: the lame, the blind, the crippled, the dumb and many others. They put them at Jesus' feet, and he healed them.

Matthew 15:31-38

31 The crowd was amazed when they saw that people who could not speak were able to speak again. The crippled were made strong again. Those who could not walk were able to walk again. The blind were able to see again. And they praised the God of Israel for this.

More than 4,000 People Fed

32 Jesus called his followers to him and said,

33 His followers asked him,

"I feel sorry for these people. They have been with me three days, and now they have nothing to eat. I don't want to send them away hungry. They might faint while going home."

"Where can we get enough bread to feed all these people? We are far away from any town."

34 Jesus asked,

"How many loaves of bread do you have?"

They answered,

"We have seven loaves and a few small fish."

35 Jesus told the people to sit on the ground. 36 He took the seven loaves of bread and the fish and gave thanks to God for the food. Then Jesus divided the food and gave it to his followers.

They gave the food to the people. 37 All the people ate and were satisfied. After this, the followers filled seven baskets with the pieces of food that were not eaten.

38 There were about 4,000 men there who ate, besides women and children.

39 After they ate, Jesus told the people to go home. He got into the boat and went to the area of Magadan.

Chapter 16

The Leaders Ask for a Miracle

1 The Pharisees[d] and Sadducees[d] came to Jesus. They wanted to trap him. So they asked him to show them a miracle[d] to prove that he was from God.

2 Jesus answered,[n]

"When you see the sunset, you know what the weather will be. If the sky is red, then you say we will have good weather.

3 And in the morning if the sky is dark and red, then you say that it will be a rainy day. You see these signs in the sky, and you know what they mean. In the same way, you see the things that are happening now. But you don't know their meaning. 4 Evil and sinful people ask for a miracle as a sign. But they will have no sign—only the sign of Jonah."[n]

Then Jesus left them and went away.

Guard Against Wrong Teachings

5 Jesus and his followers went across the lake. But the followers forgot to bring bread. 6 Jesus said to them,

"Be careful! Guard against the yeast of the Pharisees[d] and the Sadducees."[d]

7 The followers discussed the meaning of this. They said,

"Did Jesus say this because we forgot to bring bread?"

8 Jesus knew that they were talking about this. So he asked them,

"Why are you talking about not having bread? Your faith is small. 9 You still don't understand? Remember the five loaves of bread that fed the 5,000 people? And remember that you filled many baskets with bread after the people finished eating?

10 And remember the seven loaves of bread that fed the 4,000 people? Remember that you filled many baskets then also? 11 So I was not talking to you about bread. Why don't you understand that? I am telling you to be careful and guard against the yeast of the Pharisees and the Sadducees."

12 Then the followers understood what Jesus meant. He was not telling them to guard against the yeast used in bread. He was telling them to guard against the teaching of the Pharisees and the Sadducees.

16:2 answered Some Greek copies do not have the rest of verse 2 and verse 3.
16:4 sign of Jonah Jonah's three days in the big fish are like Jesus' three days in the tomb. The story about Jonah is in the book of Jonah.

Matthew 16:13-21

Peter Says Jesus Is the Christ

13 Jesus went to the area of Caesarea Philippi. He said to his followers,

"I am the Son of Man.[d] Who do the people say I am?"

14 They answered,

"Some people say you are John the Baptist.[d] Others say you are Elijah. And others say that you are Jeremiah or one of the prophets."[d]

15 Then Jesus asked them,

"And who do you say I am?"

16 Simon Peter answered,

"You are the Christ,[d] the Son of the living God."

17 Jesus answered,

"You are blessed, Simon son of Jonah.

No person taught you that. My Father in heaven showed you who I am. 18 So I tell you, you are Peter.[n] And I will build my church on this rock. The power of death will not be able to defeat my church. 19 I will give you the keys of the kingdom of heaven. The things you don't allow on earth will be the things that God does not allow. The things you allow on earth will be the things that God allows."

20 Then Jesus warned his followers not to tell anyone that he was the Christ.

Jesus Says That He Must Die

21 From that time on Jesus began telling his followers that he must go to Jerusalem. He explained that the Jewish elders, the leading priests, and the teachers of the law would make him suffer many things. And he told them that he must be killed. Then, on the third day, he would be raised from death.

16:18 Peter The Greek name "Peter," like the Aramaic name "Cephas," means "rock."

22 Peter took Jesus aside and began to criticize him. Peter said,

"God save you from those things, Lord! Those things will never happen to you!"

23 Then Jesus said to Peter,

"Go away from me, Satan![a] You are not helping me! You don't care about the things of God. You care only about things that men think are important."

24 Then Jesus said to his followers,

"If anyone wants to follow me, he must say 'no' to the things he wants. He must be willing even to die on a cross, and he must follow me. 25 Whoever wants to save his life will give up true life. And whoever gives up his life for me will have true life. 26 It is worth nothing for a man to have the whole world if he loses his soul. He could never pay enough to buy back his soul.

27 The Son of Man[d] will come again with his Father's glory and with his angels. At that time, he will reward everyone for what he has done. 28 I tell you the truth. There are some people standing here who, before they die, will see the Son of Man coming with his kingdom."

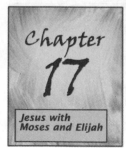

Chapter

17

Jesus with Moses and Elijah

1 Six days later, Jesus took Peter, James, and John the brother of James up on a high mountain. They were all alone there.

16:23 Satan Name for the devil, meaning "the enemy." Jesus means that Peter was talking like Satan.

Matthew 17:2-10

2 While they watched Jesus was changed. His face became bright like the sun. And his clothes became white as light.

3 Then two men were there, talking with him. The men were Moses and Elijah."

4 Peter said to Jesus,

"Lord, it is good that we are here. If you want, I will put three tents here–one for you, one for Moses, and one for Elijah."

5 While Peter was talking, a bright cloud covered them. A voice came from the cloud. The voice said,

"This is my Son and I love him. I am very pleased with him. Obey him!"

6 The followers with Jesus heard the voice. They were so fightened that they fell to the ground. 7 But Jesus went to them and touched them. He said,

"Stand up. Don't be afraid."

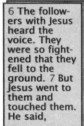

8 When the followers looked up, they saw Jesus was now alone.

9 When Jesus and the followers were coming down the mountain, Jesus commanded them,

"Don't tell anyone about the things you saw on the mountain. Wait until the Son of Man⁴ has been raised from death. Then you may tell."

10 The followers asked Jesus,

"Why do the teachers of the law say that Elijah must come first before Christ⁴ comes?"

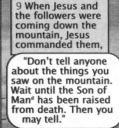

17:3 Moses and Elijah Two of the most important Jewish leaders in the past.

11 Jesus answered,

"They are right to say that Elijah is coming. And it is true that Elijah will make everything the way it should be. 12 But I tell you, Elijah has already come. People did not know who he was. They did to him everything they wanted to do. It will be the same with the Son of Man. Those same people will make the Son of Man suffer."

13 Then the followers understood that Jesus was talking about John the Baptist.[d]

Jesus Heals a Sick Boy

14 Jesus and his followers went back to the crowd. A man came to Jesus and bowed before him. 15 The man said,

"Lord, please help my son. He has epilepsy[n] and is suffering very much. He often falls into the fire or into the water. 16 I brought him to your followers, but they could not cure him."

17 Jesus answered,

"You people have no faith. Your lives are all wrong. How long must I stay with you? How long must I continue to be patient with you? Bring the boy here."

18 Jesus gave a strong command to the demon[d] inside the boy. Then the demon came out,

and the boy was healed.

19 The followers came to Jesus when he was alone. They said,

"Why couldn't we force the demon out?"

20 Jesus answered,

"You were not able to drive out the demon because your faith is too small. I tell you the truth. If your faith is as big as a mustard seed,[n] you can say to this mountain, 'Move from here to there.' And the mountain will move."

17:15 epilepsy A disease that causes a person sometimes to lose control of his body, and maybe faint, shake strongly, or not be able to move.
17:20 mustard seed This seed is very small, but the plant grows taller than a man.

Matthew 17:21-27

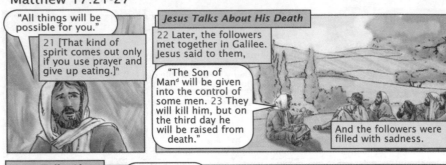

"All things will be possible for you."

21 [That kind of spirit comes out only if you use prayer and give up eating.]"

Jesus Talks About His Death

22 Later, the followers met together in Galilee. Jesus said to them,

"The Son of Man[d] will be given into the control of some men. 23 They will kill him, but on the third day he will be raised from death."

And the followers were filled with sadness.

Jesus Talks About Paying Taxes

24 Jesus and his followers went to Capernaum. There some men came to Peter. They were the men who collected the Temple[d] tax. They asked,

"Does your teacher pay the Temple tax?"

25 Peter answered,

"Yes, Jesus pays the tax."

Peter went into the house where Jesus was.

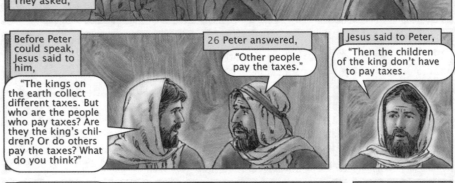

Before Peter could speak, Jesus said to him,

"The kings on the earth collect different taxes. But who are the people who pay taxes? Are they the king's children? Or do others pay the taxes? What do you think?"

26 Peter answered,

"Other people pay the taxes."

Jesus said to Peter,

"Then the children of the king don't have to pay taxes.

27 But we don't want to make these tax collectors angry. So go to the lake and fish. After you catch the first fish, open its mouth. Inside its mouth you will find a coin. Take that coin and give it to the tax collectors. That will pay the tax for you and me."

Chapter
18

17:21 That . . . eating. Some Greek copies do not contain the bracketed text.

Who Is the Greatest?

1 At that time the followers came to Jesus and asked,

"Who is greatest in the kingdom of heaven?"

2 Jesus called a little child to him. He stood the child before the followers. 3 Then he said,

"I tell you the truth. You must change and become like little children. If you don't do this, you will never enter the kingdom of heaven. 4 The greatest person in the kingdom of heaven is the one who makes himself humble like this child.

5 "Whoever accepts a little child in my name accepts me. 6 If one of these little children believes in me, and someone causes that child to sin, then it will be very bad for that person. It would be better for him to have a large stone tied around his neck and be drowned in the sea. 7 How terrible for the people of the world because of the things that cause them to sin. Such things will happen. But how terrible for the one who causes them to happen. 8 If your hand or your foot causes you to sin, cut it off and throw it away. It is better for you to have only part of your body but have life forever. That is much better than to have two hands and two feet but be thrown into the fire that burns forever. 9 If your eye causes you to sin, take it out and throw it away. It is better for you to have only one eye but have life forever. That is much better than to have two eyes but be thrown into the fire of hell.

A Lost Sheep

10 "Be careful. Don't think these little children are worth nothing. I tell you that they have angels in heaven who are always with my Father in heaven. 11 [The Son of Man came to save lost people.][n]
12 "If a man has 100 sheep, but 1 of the sheep gets lost, he will leave the other 99 sheep on the hill. He will go to look for the lost sheep. 13 And if he finds it, he is happier about that 1 sheep than about the 99 that were never lost. I tell you the truth.

18:11 The . . . people. Some Greek copies do not contain the bracketed text.

14 "In the same way, your Father in heaven does not want any of these little children to be lost.

When a Person Sins Against You

15 "If your brother sins against you,[n] go and tell him what he did wrong. Do this in private. If he listens to you, then you have helped him to be your brother again. 16 But if he refuses to listen, then go to him again and take one or two other people with you. 'Every case may be proved by two or three witnesses.'[n] 17 If he refuses to listen to them, then tell it to the church. If he refuses to listen to the church, then treat him as you would one who does not believe in God. Treat him as if he were a tax collector. 18 "I tell you the truth. The things you don't allow on earth will be the things God does not allow. The things you allow on earth will be the things that God allows. 19 "Also, I tell you that if two of you on earth agree about something, then you can pray for it. And the thing you ask for will be done for you by my Father in heaven.

20 This is true because if two or three people come together in my name, I am there with them."

An Unforgiving Servant

21 Then Peter came to Jesus and asked,

"Lord, when my brother sins against me, how many times must I forgive him? Should I forgive him as many as 7 times?"

22 Jesus answered,

"I tell you, you must forgive him more than 7 times. You must forgive him even if he does wrong to you 70 times 7.

23 "The kingdom of heaven is like a king who decided to collect the money his servants owed him. 24 So the king began to collect his money. One servant owed him several million dollars. 25 But the servant did not have enough money to pay his master, the king. So the master ordered that every- thing the servant owned should be sold, even the servant's wife and children. The money would be used to pay the king what the servant owed.

18:15 **against you** Some Greek copies do not have "against you."
18:16 **'Every . . . witnesses.'** Quotation from Deuteronomy 19:15.

26 "But the servant fell on his knees and begged,

'Be patient with me. I will pay you everything I owe.'

27 The master felt sorry for his servant. So the master told the servant he did not have to pay. He let the servant go free.
28 "Later, that same servant found another servant who owed him a few dollars. The servant grabbed the other servant around the neck and said,

'Pay me the money you owe me!'

29 "The other servant fell on his knees and begged him,

'Be patient with me. I will pay you everything I owe.'

30 "But the first servant refused to be patient. He threw the other servant into prison until he could pay everything he owed. 31 All the other servants saw what happened. They were very sorry. So they went and told their master all that had happened.

32 "Then the master called his servant in and said,

'You evil servant! You begged me to forget what you owed. So I told you that you did not have to pay anything. 33 I had mercy on you. You should have had the same mercy on that other servant.'

34 The master was very angry, and he put the servant in prison to be punished. The servant had to stay in prison until he could pay everything he owed.
35 "This king did what my heavenly Father will do to you if you do not forgive your brother from your heart."

Chapter

19

Jesus Teaches About Divorce

1 After Jesus said all these things, he left Galilee. He went into the area of Judea on the other side of the Jordan River.
2 Large crowds followed Jesus, and he healed them there.

Matthew 19:3-12

19:4 **'he made . . . female.'** Quotation from Genesis 1:27 or 5:2.
19:5 **'So . . . body.'** Quotation from Genesis 2:24. **19:9 adultery** Some Greek copies continue, "And anyone who marries a divorced woman is guilty of adultery." Compare Matthew 5:32. **19:12 But . . . marriage.** This may also mean, "The person who can accept this teaching about not marrying should accept it."

56

Jesus Welcomes Children

13 Then the people brought their little children to Jesus so that he could put his hands on them[n] and pray for them. When his followers saw this, they told the people to stop bringing their children to Jesus.

14 But Jesus said,

"Let the little children come to me. Don't stop them, because the kingdom of heaven belongs to people who are like these children."

15 After Jesus put his hands on the children, he left there.

A Rich Young Man's Question

16 A man came to Jesus and asked,

"Teacher, what good thing must I do to have life forever?"

17 Jesus answered,

"Why do you ask me about what is good? Only God is good. But if you want to have life forever, obey the commands."

18 The man asked,

"Which commands?"

Jesus answered,

" 'You must not murder anyone. You must not be guilty of adultery.[d] You must not steal. You must not tell lies about your neighbor in court. 19 Honor your father and mother.'[n] Love your neighbor as you love yourself.' "[n]

19:13 **put his hands on them** Showing that Jesus gave special blessings to these children.
19:18-19 **'You . . . mother.'** Quotation from Exodus 20:12-16; Deuteronomy 5:16-20.
19:19 **'Love . . . yourself.'** Quotation from Leviticus 19:18.

20 The young man said,

"I have obeyed all these things. What else do I need to do?"

21 Jesus answered,

"If you want to be perfect, then go and sell all the things you own. Give the money to the poor. If you do this, you will have a treasure in heaven. Then come and follow me!"

22 But when the young man heard this, he became very sad because he was very rich. So he left Jesus.

23 Then Jesus said to his followers,

"I tell you the truth. It will be very hard for a rich person to enter the kingdom of heaven. 24 Yes, I tell you that it is easier for a camel to go through the eye of a needle than for a rich person to enter the kingdom of God."

25 When the followers heard this, they were very surprised. They asked,

"Then who can be saved?"

26 Jesus looked at them and said,

"For men this is impossible. But for God all things are possible."

27 Peter said to Jesus,

"We left everything we had and followed you. So what will we have?"

28 Jesus said to them,

"I tell you the truth. When the new age comes, the Son of Man[d] will sit on his great throne. And all of you who followed me will also sit on 12 thrones. And you will judge the 12 tribes[d] of Israel. 29 And everyone who has left houses, brothers, sisters, father, mother,[n] children, or farms to follow me will get much more than he left. And he will have life forever. 30 Many who are first now will be last in the future. And many who are last now will be first in the future."

19:29 mother Some Greek copies continue, "or wife."

Chapter 20

A Story About Vineyard Workers

1 "The kingdom of heaven is like a man who owned some land. One morning, he went out very early to hire some people to work in his vineyard. 2 The man agreed to pay the workers one silver coin[n] for working that day. Then he sent them into the vineyard to work. 3 About nine o'clock the man went to the marketplace and saw some other people standing there, doing nothing. 4 So he said to them,

'If you go and work in my vineyard, I will pay you what your work is worth.'

5 So they went to work in the vineyard. The man went out again about twelve o'clock and again at three o'clock. Both times he hired people to work in his vineyard. 6 About five o'clock the man went to the marketplace again. He saw others standing there. He asked them,

'Why did you stand here all day doing nothing?'

7 They answered,

'No one gave us a job.'

The man said to them, 'Then you can go and work in my vineyard.'
8 "At the end of the day, the owner of the vineyard said to the boss of all the workers,

'Call the workers and pay them. Start by paying the last people I hired. Then pay all of them, ending with the workers I hired first.'

9 "The workers who were hired at five o'clock came to get their pay. Each worker received one silver coin. 10 Then the workers who were hired first came to get their pay. They thought they would be paid more than the others. But each one of them also received one silver coin. 11 When they got their silver coin, they complained to the man who owned the land. 12 They said,

'Those people were hired last and worked only one hour. But you paid them the same as you paid us. And we worked hard all day in the hot sun.'

13 But the man who owned the vineyard said to one of those workers,

'Friend, I am being fair to you. You agreed to work for one silver coin. 14 So take your pay and go. I want to give the man who was hired last the same pay that I gave you. 15 I can do what I want with my own money. Are you jealous because I am good to those people?'

20:2 silver coin A Roman denarius. One coin was the average pay for one day's work.

16 "So those who are last now will someday be first. And those who are first now will someday be last."

Jesus Talks About His Own Death

17 Jesus was going to Jerusalem. His 12 followers were with him. While they were on the way, Jesus gathered the followers together and spoke to them privately. He said to them,

18 "We are going to Jerusalem. The Son of Man[d] will be turned over to the leading priests and the teachers of the law. They will say that he must die. 19 They will give the Son of Man to the non-Jewish people. They will laugh at him and beat him with whips, and then they will kill him on a cross. But on the third day after his death, he will be raised to life again."

A Mother Asks Jesus a Favor

20 Then the wife of Zebedee came to Jesus. Her sons were with her. The mother bowed before Jesus and asked him to do something for her. 21 Jesus asked,

"What do you want?"

She said,

"Promise that one of my sons will sit at your right side in your kingdom. And promise that the other son will sit at your left side."

22 But Jesus said,

"You don't understand what you are asking. Can you accept the kind of suffering that I must suffer?"[n]

The sons answered,

"Yes, we can!"

23 Jesus said to them,

"Truly you will suffer the same things that I will suffer. But I cannot choose who will sit at my right side or my left side. Those places belong to those for whom my Father has prepared them."

24 The other ten followers heard this and were angry with the two brothers.

25 Jesus called all the followers together. He said,

"You know that the rulers of the non-Jewish people love to show their power over the people. And their important leaders love to use all their authority. 26 But it should not be that way among you. If one of you wants to become great, then he must serve the rest of you like a servant.

20:22 accept . . . suffer Literally, "drink the cup that I must drink." Jesus used the idea of drinking from a cup to mean accepting the terrible things that would happen to him.

27 "If one of you wants to become first, then he must serve the rest of you like a slave. 28 So it is with the Son of Man.[d] The Son of Man did not come for other people to serve him. He came to serve others. The Son of Man came to give his life to save many people."

Jesus Heals Two Blind Men

29 When Jesus and his followers were leaving Jericho, a great many people followed Jesus.

30 There were two blind men sitting by the road. The blind men heard that Jesus was going by, so they shouted,

"Lord, Son of David,[d] please help us!"

31 All the people criticized the blind men. They told them to be quiet. But the blind men shouted more and more,

"Lord, Son of David, please help us!"

32 Jesus stopped and said to the blind men,

"What do you want me to do for you?"

33 They answered,

"Lord, we want to be able to see."

34 Jesus felt sorry for the blind men. He touched their eyes,

and at once they were able to see. Then the men followed Jesus.

Chapter

21

Jesus Enters Jerusalem as a King

1 Jesus and his followers were coming closer to Jerusalem. But first they stopped at Bethphage at the hill called the Mount of Olives.[d] From there Jesus sent two of his followers into the town. 2 He said to them,

"Go to the town you can see there. When you enter it, you will find a donkey tied there with its colt. Untie them and bring them to me.

Matthew 21:3-11

3 "If anyone asks you why you are taking the donkeys, tell him, 'The Master needs them. He will send them back soon.' "

4 This was to make clear the full meaning of what the prophet[d] said:

5 "Tell the people of Jerusalem, 'Your king is coming to you. He is gentle and riding on a donkey. He is on the colt of a donkey.' "
Isaiah 62:11; Zechariah 9:9

6 The followers went and did what Jesus told them to do. 7 They brought the donkey and the colt to Jesus. They laid their coats on the donkeys, and Jesus sat on them.

8 Many people spread their coats on the road before Jesus. Others cut branches from the trees and spread them on the road. 9 Some of the people were walking ahead of Jesus. Others were walking behind him. All the people were shouting,

"Praise[n] to the Son of David![d] God bless the One who comes in the name of the Lord!
Psalm 118:26

Praise to God in heaven!"

10 Then Jesus went into Jerusalem. The city was filled with excitement. The people asked,

"Who is this man?"

11 The crowd answered,

"This man is Jesus. He is the prophet from the town of Nazareth in Galilee."

21:9 Praise Literally, "Hosanna," a Hebrew word used at first in praying to God for help. At this time it was probably a shout of joy used in praising God or his Messiah.

62

Jesus Goes to the Temple

12 Jesus went into the Temple.[d] He threw out all the people who were buying and selling there. He turned over the tables that belonged to the men who were exchanging different kinds of money. And he upset the benches of those who were selling doves. 13 Jesus said to all the people there,

"It is written in the Scriptures,[d] 'My Temple will be a house where people will pray.'[n] But you are changing God's house into a 'hideout for robbers.' "[n]

14 The blind and crippled people came to Jesus in the Temple, and Jesus healed them. 15 The leading priests and the teachers of the law saw that Jesus was doing wonderful things. They saw the children praising him in the Temple. The children were saying,

"Praise[n] to the Son of David."[d]

All these things made the priests and the teachers of the law very angry. 16 They asked Jesus,

"Do you hear the things these children are saying?"

Jesus answered,

"Yes. Haven't you read in the Scriptures, 'You have taught children and babies to sing praises'?"[n]

17 Then Jesus left and went out of the city to Bethany, where he spent the night.

The Power of Faith

18 Early the next morning, Jesus was going back to the city. He was very hungry. 19 He saw a fig tree beside the road. Jesus went to it, but there were no figs on the tree. There were only leaves. So Jesus said to the tree,

"You will never again have fruit!"

The tree immediately dried up. 20 His followers saw this and were amazed. They asked,

---

21:13 'My Temple . . . pray.' Quotation from Isaiah 56:7. **21:13 'hideout for robbers.'** Quotation from Jeremiah 7:11. **21:15 Praise** Literally, "Hosanna," a Hebrew word used at first in praying to God for help. At this time it was probably a shout of joy used in praising God or his Messiah. **21:16 'You . . . praises'** Quotation from the Septuagint (Greek) version of Psalm 8:2. 63

Matthew 21:21-27

"How did the fig tree dry up so quickly?"

21 Jesus answered,

"I tell you the truth. If you have faith and do not doubt, you will be able to do what I did to this tree. And you will be able to do more. You will be able to say to this mountain, 'Go, mountain, fall into the sea.' And if you have faith, it will happen."

22 If you believe, you will get anything you ask for in prayer."

Leaders Doubt Jesus' Authority

23 Jesus went to the Temple.[d] While he was teaching there, the leading priests and the elders of the people came to Jesus. They said to him,

"Tell us! What authority do you have to do these things? Who gave you this authority?"

24 Jesus answered,

"I will ask you a question, too. If you answer me, then I will tell you what authority I have to do these things. 25 Tell me: When John baptized people, did that come from God or from man?"

The priests and the leaders argued about Jesus' question. They said to each other,

"If we answer, 'John's baptism was from God,' then Jesus will say, 'Then why didn't you believe John?' 26 But if we say, 'It was from man,' we are afraid of what the people will do because they all believe that John was a prophet."[d]

"We don't know."

27 So they answered Jesus,

Then Jesus said,

"Then I won't tell you what authority I have to do these things!

A Story About Two Sons

28 "Tell me what you think about this: There was a man who had two sons. He went to the first son and said,

'Son, go and work today in my vineyard.'

29 The son answered,

'I will not go.'

But later the son decided he should go, and he went.

30 Then the father went to the other son and said, 'Son, go and work today in my vineyard.' The son answered,

'Yes, sir, I will go and work.'

But he did not go.

31 Which of the two sons obeyed his father?"

The priests and leaders answered,

"The first son."

Jesus said to them,

"I tell you the truth. The tax collectors and the prostitutes[d] will enter the kingdom of God before you do. 32 John came to show you the right way to live. And you did not believe him. But the tax collectors and prostitutes believed John.

You saw this, but you still refused to change and believe him.

God Sends His Son

33 "Listen to this story: There was a man who owned a vineyard. He put a wall around the vineyard and dug a hole for a winepress.[d] Then he built a tower. He leased the land to some farmers and left for a trip.

65

grabbed the servants, beat one, killed another, and then killed a third servant with stones.

36 So the man sent some other servants to the farmers. He sent more servants than he sent the first time. But the farmers did the same thing to the servants that they had done before.

37 So the man decided to send his son to the farmers. He said, 'The farmers will respect my son.' 38 But when the farmers saw the son, they said to each other,

'This is the owner's son. This vineyard will be his. If we kill him, then his vineyard will be ours!'

34 "Later, it was time for the grapes to be picked. So the man sent his servants to the farmers to get his share of the grapes. 35 But the farmers

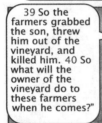

39 So the farmers grabbed the son, threw him out of the vineyard, and killed him. 40 So what will the owner of the vineyard do to these farmers when he comes?"

41 The priests and leaders said,

"He will surely kill those evil men. Then he will lease the vineyard to some other farmers. They will give him his share of the crop at harvest time."

42 Jesus said to them,

"Surely you have read this in the Scriptures:ᵈ

'The stone that the builders did not want became the cornerstone.ᵈ The Lord did this, and it is wonderful to us.'
Psalm 118:22-23

43 "So I tell you that the kingdom of God will be taken away from you. It will be given to people who do the things God wants in his kingdom.

44 "The person who falls on this stone will be broken. But if the stone falls on him, he will be crushed."[n]

45 The leading priests and the Pharisees[d] heard these stories that Jesus told. They knew he was talking about them. 46 They wanted to arrest him. But they were afraid of the people, because the people believed that Jesus was a prophet.[d]

Chapter 22

A Story About a Wedding Feast

1 Jesus used stories to tell other things to the people. He said,

2 "The kingdom of heaven is like a king who prepared a wedding feast for his son.

3 The king invited some people to the feast. When the feast was ready, the king sent his servants to tell the people to come. But they refused to come to the feast.

4 "Then the king sent other servants. He said to them,

'Tell those who have been invited that my feast is ready. I have killed my best bulls and calves for the dinner. Everything is ready. Come to the wedding feast.'

5 "But the people refused to listen to the servants. They went to do other things. One went to work in his field, and another went to his business.

6 Some of the other people grabbed the servants, beat them, and killed them.

7 The king was very angry. He sent his army to kill the people who had killed his servants. And the army burned their city.

21:44 The . . . crushed. Some Greek copies do not have verse 44.

Matthew 22:8-18

8 "After that, the king said to his servants,

'The wedding feast is ready. I invited those people, but they were not worthy to come. 9 So go to the street corners and invite everyone you see. Tell them to come to my feast.'

10 "So the servants went into the streets. They gathered all the people they could find, both good and bad. And the wedding hall was filled with guests.

11 "Then the king came in . to see all the guests. He saw a man there who was not dressed in the right clothes for a wedding. 12 The king said,

'Friend, how were you allowed to come in here? You are not wearing the right clothes for a wedding.'

But the man said nothing.

13 So the king told some servants,

'Tie this man's hands and feet. Throw him out into the darkness. In that place, people will cry and grind their teeth with pain.'

14 "Yes, many are invited. But only a few are chosen."

The Pharisees Try to Trap Jesus

15 Then the Pharisees^d left the place where Jesus was teaching. They made plans to trap Jesus with a question.

16 They sent some of their own followers and some men from the group called Herodians.ⁿ These men said,

"Teacher, we know that you are an honest man. We know that you teach the truth about God's way. You are not afraid of what other people think about you. All men are the same to you. 17 So tell us what you think. Is it right to pay taxes to Caesar^d or not?"

18 But Jesus knew that these men were trying to trick him. So he said,

22:16 Herodians A political group that followed Herod and his family.

68

"You hypocrites![d] Why are you trying to trap me? 19 Show me a coin used for paying the tax."

The men showed him a silver coin.[n] 20 Then Jesus asked,

"Whose picture is on the coin? And whose name is written on the coin?"

21 The men answered,

"Caesar's."

Then Jesus said to them,

"Give to Caesar the things that are Caesar's. And give to God the things that are God's."

22 The men heard what Jesus said, and they were amazed. They left him and went away.

Sadducees Try to Trick Jesus

23 That same day some Sadducees[d] came to Jesus. (Sadducees believe that no person will rise from death.) The Sadducees asked Jesus a question. 24 They said,

"Teacher, Moses told us that a married man might die without having children. Then his brother must marry the widow and have children for him.

25 There were seven brothers among us. The first one married but died. He had no children. So his brother married the widow. 26 Then the second brother also died. The same thing happened to the third brother and all the other brothers. 27 The woman was last to die. 28 But all seven men had married her. So when people rise from death, whose wife will she be?"

22:19 silver coin A Roman denarius. One coin was the average pay for one day's work.

29 Jesus answered,

"You don't understand because you don't know what the Scriptures[d] say. And you don't know about the power of God. **30** When people rise from death, there will be no marriage. People will not be married to each other. They will be like the angels in heaven. **31** Surely you have read what God said to you about the rising from death? **32** God said, 'I am the God of Abraham, the God of Isaac, and the God of Jacob.'[n] God is the God of living people, not dead people."

33 All the people heard this. They were amazed at Jesus' teaching.

The Most Important Command

34 The Pharisees[d] learned that the Sadducees[d] could not argue with Jesus' answers to them. So the Pharisees met together. **35** One Pharisee was an expert in the law of Moses. That Pharisee asked Jesus a question to test him. **36** The Pharisee asked,

"Teacher, which command in the law is the most important?"

37 Jesus answered,

" 'Love the Lord your God with all your heart, soul and mind.'[n] **38** This is the first and most important command. **39** And the second command is like the first: 'Love your neighbor as you love yourself.'[n] **40** All the law and the writings of the prophets[d] depend on these two commands."

22:32 'I am . . . Jacob.' Quotation from Exodus 3:6.
22:37 'Love . . . mind.' Quotation from Deuteronomy 6:5.
22:39 'Love . . . yourself.' Quotation from Leviticus 19:18.

Jesus Questions the Pharisees

41 While the Pharisees[d] were together, Jesus asked them a question.

42 He asked, "What do you think about the Christ?[d] Whose son is he?"

The Pharisees answered,

"The Christ is the Son of David."[d]

43 Then Jesus said to them,

"Then why did David call him 'Lord'? David was speaking by the power of the Holy Spirit.[d] David said,

44 'The Lord said to my Lord: Sit by me at my right side, until I put your enemies under your control.'

Psalm 110:1

45 David calls the Christ 'Lord.' So how can he be David's son?"

46 None of the Pharisees could answer Jesus' question. And after that day no one was brave enough to ask Jesus any more questions.

Chapter 23

Jesus Accuses the Leaders

1 Then Jesus spoke to the crowds and to his followers. Jesus said,

2 "The teachers of the law and the Pharisees[d] have the authority to tell you what the law of Moses says. 3 So you should obey and follow whatever they tell you. But their lives are not good examples for you to follow. They tell you to do things, but they don't do the things themselves. 4 They make strict rules and try to force people to obey them. But they themselves will not try to follow any of those rules.

5 "The reason they do good things is so other people will see them. They make the boxes[n] of Scriptures[d] that they wear bigger and bigger. And they make their special prayer clothes very long so that people will notice them. 6 Those Pharisees and teachers of the law love to have the most important seats at the feasts. And they love to have the most important seats in the synagogues.[d] 7 They love people to show respect to them in the marketplaces. And they love to have people call them 'Teacher.'

23:5 boxes Small leather boxes containing four important Scriptures. Some Jews tied these to the forehead and left arm, probably to show they were very religious.

8 "But you must not be called 'Teacher.' You are all brothers and sisters together. You have only one Teacher. 9 And don't call any person on earth 'Father.' You have one Father. He is in heaven. 10 And you should not be called 'Master.' You have only one Master, the Christ.[d] 11 He who serves you as a servant is the greatest among you. 12 Whoever makes himself great will be made humble. Whoever makes himself humble will be made great.

13 "How terrible for you, teachers of the law and Pharisees! You are hypocrites![d] You close the door for people to enter the kingdom of heaven. You yourselves don't enter, and you stop others who are trying to enter. 14 [How terrible for you, teachers of the law and Pharisees. You are hypocrites. You take away widows' houses, and you make long prayers so that people can see you. So you will have a worse punishment.][n] 15 "How terrible for you, teachers of the law and Pharisees! You are hypocrites! You travel across land and sea to find one person who will follow your ways. When you find that person, you make him more fit for hell than you are.

16 "How terrible for you, teachers of the law and Pharisees! You guide the people, but you are blind. You say, 'If anyone swears by the Temple[d] when he makes a promise, that means nothing. But if anyone swears by the gold that is in the Temple, then he must keep that promise.' 17 You are blind fools! Which is greater: the gold or the Temple? The Temple makes that gold holy. 18 And you say, 'If anyone swears by the altar when he makes a promise, that means nothing. But if he swears by the gift on the altar, then he must keep his promise.' 19 You are blind! Which is greater: the gift or the altar? The altar makes the gift holy. 20 The person who swears by the altar is really using the altar and also everything on the altar. 21 And the person who uses the Temple to make a promise is really using the Temple and also everything in the Temple. 22 The person who uses heaven to make a promise is also using God's throne and the One who sits on that throne.

23 "How terrible for you, teachers of the law and Pharisees! You are hypocrites! You give to God one-tenth of everything you earn—even your mint, dill, and cummin.[n] But you don't obey the really important teachings of the law—being fair, showing mercy, and being loyal. These are the things you should do, as well as those other things.

23:14 How . . . punishment. Some Greek copies do not contain the bracketed text.
23:23 mint, dill, and cummin Small plants grown in gardens and used for spices. Only very religious people would be careful enough to give a tenth of these plants.

24 "You guide the people, but you are blind! You are like a person who picks a fly out of his drink and then swallows a camel![n]
25 "How terrible for you, teachers of the law and Pharisees! You are hypocrites! You wash the outside of your cups and dishes. But inside they are full of things that you got by cheating others and pleasing only yourselves. 26 Pharisees, you are blind! First make the inside of the cup clean and good. Then the outside of the cup can be truly clean.
27 "How terrible for you, teachers of the law and Pharisees! You are hypocrites! You are like tombs that are painted white. Outside, those tombs look fine. But inside, they are full of the bones of dead people, and all kinds of unclean things are there. 28 It is the same with you. People look at you and think you are good. But on the inside you are full of hypocrisy and evil.

29 "How terrible for you, teachers of the law and Pharisees! You are hypocrites! You build tombs for the prophets.[d] You show honor to the graves of people who lived good lives. 30 And you say, 'If we had lived during the time of our fathers, we would not have helped them kill the prophets.' 31 But you give proof that you are children of those people who murdered the prophets. 32 And you will complete the sin that your fathers started! 33 "You are snakes! A family of poisonous snakes! You will not escape God. You will all be judged guilty and be sent to hell! 34 So I tell you this: I am sending to you prophets and wise men and teachers. You will kill some of these people. You will nail some of them to crosses. You will beat some of them in your synagogues. You will chase them from town to town. 35 So you will be guilty for the death of all the good people who have been

killed on earth. You will be guilty for the murder of that good man Abel. And you will be guilty for the murder of Zechariah[n] son of Berakiah. He was murdered when he was between the Temple and the altar. 36 I tell you the truth. All of these things will happen to you people who are living now.

Jesus Feels Sorry for Jerusalem

37 "Jerusalem, Jerusalem! You kill the prophets[d] and kill with stones those men God sent to you. Many times I wanted to help your people! I wanted to gather them together as a hen gathers her chicks under her wings. But you did not let me. 38 Now your home will be left completely empty. 39 I tell you, you will not see me again until that time when you will say, 'God bless the One who comes in the name of the Lord.' "[n]

23:24 You . . . camel! Meaning, "You worry about the smallest mistakes but commit the biggest sin." **23:35 Abel . . . Zechariah** In the Hebrew Old Testament, the first and last men to be murdered. **23:39 'God . . . Lord.'** Quotation from Psalm 118:26.

Chapter 24

The Temple Will Be Destroyed

1 Jesus left the Temple[d] and was walking away. But his followers came to show him the Temple's buildings. 2 Jesus asked,

"Do you see all these buildings? I tell you the truth. Every stone will be thrown down to the ground. Not one stone will be left on another."

3 Later, Jesus was sitting on the Mount of Olives.[d] His followers came to be alone with him. They said,

"Tell us when these things will happen. And what will happen to show us that it is time for you to come again and for the world to end?"

4 Jesus answered:

"Be careful that no one fools you. 5 Many people will come in my name. They will say, 'I am the Christ.'[d] And they will fool many people. 6 You will hear about wars and stories of wars that are coming. But don't be afraid. These things must happen before the end comes. 7 Nations will fight against other nations. Kingdoms will fight against other kingdoms. There will be times when there is no food for people to eat. And there will be earthquakes in different places. 8 These things are like the first pains when something new is about to be born. 9 "Then men will arrest you and hand you over to be hurt and kill you. They will hate you because you believe in me.

10 "At that time, many who believe will lose their faith. They will turn against each other and hate each other. 11 Many false prophets[d] will come and cause many people to believe false things. 12 There will be more and more evil in the world. So most people will stop showing their love for each other. 13 But the person who continues to be strong until the end will be saved. 14 The Good News[d] about God's kingdom will be preached in all the world, to every nation. Then the end will come.

15 "Daniel the prophet spoke about 'the horrible thing that destroys.'[n] You will see this terrible thing standing in the holy place." (You who read this should understand what it means.) 16 "At that time, the people in Judea should run away to the mountains. 17 If a person is on the roof[n] of his house, he must not go down to get anything out of his house. 18 If a person is in the field, he must not go back to get his coat. 19 At that time, it will be hard for women who are pregnant or have nursing babies! 20 Pray that it will not be winter or a Sabbath[d] day when these things happen and you have to run away. 21 This is

because at that time there will be much trouble. There will be more trouble than has ever happened since the beginning of the world. And nothing as bad as that will ever happen again. 22 God has decided to make that terrible time short. If that time were not made short, then no one would go on living. But God will make that time short to help the people he has chosen. 23 At that time, someone might say to you, 'Look, there is the Christ!' Or another person might say, 'There he is!' But don't believe them. 24 False Christs and false prophets will come and perform great things and miracles.[d] They will do these things to the people God has chosen. They will fool them, if that is possible. 25 Now I have warned you about this before it happens. 26 "If people tell you, 'The Christ is in the desert'— don't go there. If they say, 'The Christ is in the inner room'—don't believe it. 27 When the Son of Man[d] comes, he will be seen by everyone. It will be like lightning flashing in the sky that can be seen everywhere. 28 Wherever there is a dead body, there the vultures will gather. 29 "Soon after the trouble of those days, this will happen:

'The sun will grow dark. And the moon will not give its light. The stars will fall from the sky. And everything in the sky will be changed.'
        Isaiah 13:10; 34:4

30 "At that time, there will be something in the sky that shows the Son of Man is coming. All the peoples of the world will cry. They will see the Son of Man coming on clouds in the sky. He will come with great power and glory. 31 He will use a loud trumpet to send his angels all around the earth. They will gather his chosen people from every part of the world.

32 "The fig tree teaches us a lesson: When its branches become green and soft, and new leaves begin to grow, then you know that summer is near. 33 So also, when you see all these things happening, you will know that the time is near, ready to come. 34 I tell you the truth. All these things will happen while the people of this time are still living! 35 The whole world, earth and sky, will be destroyed, but the words I have said will never be destroyed!

When Will Jesus Come Again?

36 "No one knows when that day or time will be. Even the Son[n] and the angels in heaven don't know. Only the Father knows. 37 When the Son of Man[d] comes, it will be the same as what happened during Noah's time. 38 In those days before the flood, people were eating and drinking. They were marrying and giving their children to be married. They were still doing those things until the day Noah entered the boat.

24:15 'the horrible . . . destroys.' Mentioned in Daniel 9:27; 12:11 (cf. Daniel 11:31). 24:17 roof In Bible times houses were built with flat roofs. The roof was used for drying things such as flax and fruit. And it was used as an extra room, as a place for worship and as a place to sleep in the summer. 24:36 Even the Son Some Greek copies do not have this phrase. 75

39 "They knew nothing about what was happening. But then the flood came, and all those people were destroyed. It will be the same when the Son of Man comes. 40 Two men will be working together in the field. One man will be taken and the other left. 41 Two women will be grinding grain with a hand mill.[n] One woman will be taken and the other will be left.

42 "So always be ready. You don't know the day your Lord will come. 43 Remember this: If the owner of the house knew what time a thief was coming, then the owner would be ready for him. The owner would watch and not let the thief enter his house. 44 So you also must be ready. The Son of Man will come at a time you don't expect him.

45 "Who is the wise and trusted servant? The master trusts one servant to give the other servants their food at the right time. 46 When the master comes and finds the servant doing his work, the servant will be very happy. 47 I tell you the truth. The master will choose that servant to take care of everything the master owns. 48 But what will happen if the servant is evil and thinks his master will not come back soon? 49 Then that servant will begin to beat the other servants. He will feast and get drunk with others like him. 50 And the master will come when the servant is not ready and is not expecting him. 51 Then the master will punish that servant. He will send him away to be among the hypocrites.[d] There people will cry and grind their teeth with pain.

24:41 mill Two large, round, flat rocks used for grinding grain to make flour.

76

Chapter 25

A Story About Ten Girls

1 "At that time the kingdom of heaven will be like ten girls who went to wait for the bridegroom. They took their lamps with them. 2 Five of the girls were foolish and five were wise. 3 The five foolish girls took their lamps, but they did not take more oil for the lamps to burn. 4 The wise girls took their lamps and more oil in jars.

5 The bridegroom was very late. All the girls became sleepy and went to sleep.

6 "At midnight someone cried out,

'The bridegroom is coming! Come and meet him!'

7 Then all the girls woke up and got their lamps ready.

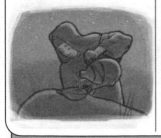

8 But the foolish girls said to the wise,

'Give us some of your oil. Our lamps are going out.'

9 The wise girls answered,

'No! The oil we have might not be enough for all of us. Go to the people who sell oil and buy some for yourselves.'

10 "So the five foolish girls went to buy oil. While they were gone, the bridegroom came. The girls who were ready went in with the bridegroom to the wedding feast. Then the door was closed and locked.

11 "Later the others came back. They called,

'Sir, sir, open the door to let us in.'

12 But the bridegroom answered,

'I tell you the truth, I don't know you.'

13 "So always be ready. You don't know the day or the time the Son of Man[d] will come.

A Story About Three Servants

14 "The kingdom of heaven is like a man who was going to another place for a visit. Before he left, he talked with his servants. The man told them to take care of his things while he was gone.

15 He decided how much each servant would be able to care for. He gave one servant five bags of money. He gave another servant two bags of money. And he gave a third servant one bag of money.

Then the man left. 16 The servant who got five bags went quickly to invest the money. The five bags of money earned five more. 17 It was the same with the servant who had two bags of money. He invested the money and earned two more. 18 But the servant who got one bag of money went out and dug a hole in the ground. Then he hid his master's money in the hole.

19 "After a long time the master came home. He asked the servants what they did with his money. 20 The servant who got five bags of money brought five more bags to the master. The servant said,

'Master, you trusted me to care for five bags of money. So I used your five bags to earn five more.'

21 The master answered,

'You did well. You are a good servant who can be trusted. You did well with small things. So I will let you care for much greater things. Come and share my happiness with me.'

22 "Then the servant who got two bags of money came to the master. The servant said,

'Master, you gave me two bags of money to care for. So I used your two bags to earn two more.'

23 "The master answered,

'You did well. You are a good servant who can be trusted. You did well with small things. So I will let you care for much greater things. Come and share my happiness with me.'

24 "Then the servant who got one bag of money came to the master. The servant said,

'Master, I knew that you were a hard man. You harvest things you did not plant. You gather crops where you did not sow any seed. 25 So I was afraid. I went and hid your money in the ground. Here is the bag of money you gave me.'

26 The master answered,

'You are a bad and lazy servant! You say you knew that I harvest things I did not plant, and that I gather crops where I did not sow any seed? 27 So you should have put my money in the bank. Then, when I came home, I would get my money back with interest.'

28 "So the master told his other servants,

'Take the bag of money from that servant and give it to the servant who has ten bags of money.

29 Everyone who uses what he has will get more. He will have much more than he needs. But the one who does not use what he has will have everything taken away from him.'

30 Then the master said,

'Throw that useless servant outside, into the darkness! There people will cry and grind their teeth with pain.'

The King Will Judge All People

31 "The Son of Man[d] will come again in his great glory. All his angels will come with him. He will be King and sit on his great throne. 32 All the people of the world will be gathered before him. Then he will separate them into two groups as a shepherd separates the sheep from the goats. 33 The Son of Man will put the sheep, the good people, on his right and the goats, the bad people, on his left.

34 "Then the King will say to the good people on his right, 'Come. My Father has given you his blessing. Come and receive the kingdom God has prepared for you since the world was made. 35 I was hungry, and you gave me food. I was thirsty, and you gave me something to drink. I was alone and away from home, and you invited me into your house. 36 I was without clothes, and you gave me something to wear. I was sick, and you cared for me. I was in prison, and you visited me.' 37 "Then the good people will answer, 'Lord, when did we see you hungry and give you food? When did we see you thirsty and give you something to drink? 38 When did we see you alone and away from home and invite you into our house? When did we see you without clothes and give you something to wear? 39 When did we see you sick or in prison and care for you?'

40 "Then the King will answer, 'I tell you the truth. Anything you did for any of my people here, you also did for me.' 41 "Then the King will say to those on his left, 'Go away from me. God has said that you will be punished. Go into the fire that burns forever. That fire was prepared for the devil and his helpers.

42 "I was hungry, and you gave me nothing to eat. I was thirsty, and you gave me nothing to drink. 43 I was alone and away from home, and you did not invite me into your house. I was without clothes, and you gave me nothing to wear. I was sick and in prison, and you did not care for me.'
44 "Then those people will answer, 'Lord, when did we see you hungry or thirsty? When did we see you alone and away from home? Or when did we see you without clothes or sick or in prison? When did we see these things and not help you?'

45 "Then the King will answer, 'I tell you the truth. Anything you refused to do for any of my people here, you refused to do for me.' 46 "These people will go off to be punished forever. But the good people will go to live forever."

Chapter 26

The Plan to Kill Jesus

1 After Jesus finished saying all these things, he told his followers,

2 "You know that the day after tomorrow is the day of the Passover[d] Feast. On that day the Son of Man[d] will be given to his enemies to be killed on a cross."

3 Then the leading priests and the Jewish elders had a meeting at the palace of the high priest. The high priest's name was Caiaphas. 4 At the meeting, they planned to set a trap to arrest Jesus and kill him. 5 But they said,

"We must not do it during the feast. The people might cause a riot."

A Woman with Perfume for Jesus

6 Jesus was in Bethany. He was at the house of Simon, who had a harmful skin disease. 7 While Jesus was there, a woman came to him. She had an alabaster[d] jar filled with expensive perfume. She poured this perfume on Jesus' head while he was eating.

8 His followers saw the woman do this and were upset. They asked,

"Why waste that perfume? 9 It could be sold for a great deal of money, and the money could be given to the poor."

10 But Jesus knew what happened. He said,

"Why are you troubling this woman? She did a very beautiful thing for me. 11 You will always have the poor with you. But you will not always have me. 12 This woman poured perfume on my body to prepare me for burial. 13 I tell you the truth. The Good News[d] will be told to people in all the world. And in every place where it is preached, what this woman has done will be told. And people will remember her."

Judas Becomes an Enemy of Jesus

14 Then 1 of the 12 followers went to talk to the leading priests. This was the follower named Judas Iscariot. 15 He said,

"I will give Jesus to you. What will you pay me for doing this?"

The priests gave Judas 30 silver coins. 16 After that, Judas waited for the best time to give Jesus to the priests.

Matthew 26:17-26

Jesus Eats the Passover Feast

17 On the first day of the Feast[d] of Unleavened Bread, the followers came to Jesus. They said,

"We will prepare everything for you to eat the Passover[d] Feast. Where do you want to have the feast?"

18 Jesus answered,

"Go into the city to a certain man. Tell him that the Teacher says, 'The chosen time is near. I will have the Passover Feast with my followers at your house.' "

19 The followers did what Jesus told them to do, and they prepared the Passover Feast.

20 In the evening Jesus was sitting at the table with his 12 followers. 21 They were all eating. Then Jesus said,

"I tell you the truth. One of you 12 will turn against me."

22 This made the followers very sad. Each one said to Jesus,

"Surely, Lord, I am not the one who will turn against you. Am I?"

23 Jesus answered,

"The man who has dipped his hand with me into the bowl is the one who will turn against me. 24 The Son of Man[d] will die. The Scriptures[d] say this will happen. But how terrible it will be for the person who gives the Son of Man to be killed. It would be better for him if he had never been born."

25 Then Judas said to Jesus,

"Teacher, surely I am not the one. Am I?"

(Judas is the one who would give Jesus to his enemies.) Jesus answered,

"Yes, it is you."

The Lord's Supper

26 While they were eating, Jesus took some bread. He thanked God for it and broke it.

Then he gave it to his followers and said,

"Take this bread and eat it. This bread is my body."

27 Then Jesus took a cup. He thanked God for it and gave it to the followers. He said,

"Every one of you drink this. 28 This is my blood which begins the new[n] agreement that God makes with his people. This blood is poured out for many to forgive their sins.

29 "I tell you this: I will not drink of this fruit of the vine[n] again until that day when I drink it new with you in my Father's kingdom."

30 They sang a hymn. Then they went out to the Mount of Olives.[d]

Jesus' Followers Will All Leave Him

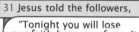
31 Jesus told the followers,

"Tonight you will lose your faith because of me. It is written in the Scriptures:[d]

'I will kill the shepherd, and the sheep will scatter.'
Zechariah 13:7

32 But after I rise from death, I will go ahead of you into Galilee."

33 Peter said,

"All the other followers may lose their faith because of you. But I will never lose my faith."

34 Jesus said,

"I tell you the truth. Tonight you will say you don't know me. You will say this three times before the rooster crows."

26:28 new Some Greek copies do not have this word. Compare Luke 22:20.
26:29 fruit of the vine Product of the grapevine; this may also be translated "wine."

Matthew 26:35-42

35 But Peter said,

"I will never say that I don't know you! I will even die with you!"

And all the other followers said the same thing.

Jesus Prays Alone

36 Then Jesus went with his followers to a place called Gethsemane. He said to them,

"Sit here while I go over there and pray."

37 He told Peter and the two sons of Zebedee to come with him. Then Jesus began to be very sad and troubled. 38 He said to Peter and the two sons of Zebedee,

"My heart is full of sorrow and breaking with sadness. Stay here with me and watch."

39 Then Jesus walked a little farther away from them. He fell to the ground and prayed,

"My Father, if it is possible, do not give me this cup of suffering. But do what you want, not what I want."

40 Then Jesus went back to his followers and found them asleep. Jesus said to Peter,

"You men could not stay awake with me for one hour? 41 Stay awake and pray for strength against temptation. Your spirit wants to do what is right. But your body is weak."

42 Then Jesus went away a second time. He prayed,

"My Father, if it is not possible for this painful thing to be taken from me, and if I must do it, then I pray that what you want will be done."

26:39 cup Jesus is talking about the bad things that will happen to him. Accepting these things will be very hard, like drinking a cup of something that tastes very bitter.

43 Then Jesus went back to the followers. Again he found them asleep, because their eyes were heavy. 44 So Jesus left them and went away one more time and prayed. This third time he prayed, he said the same thing. 45 Then Jesus went back to the followers and said,

"You are still sleeping and resting? The time has come for the Son of Man[d] to be given to sinful people.

Jesus Is Arrested

46 Get up. We must go. Here comes the man who has turned against me."

47 While Jesus was still speaking, Judas came up. Judas was 1 of the 12 followers. He had many people with him. They had been sent from the leading priests and the elders of the people. They carried swords and clubs.

48 Judas had planned to give them a signal. He had said, "The man I kiss is Jesus. Arrest him." 49 At once Judas went to Jesus and said,

"Greetings, Teacher!"

Then Judas kissed him. 50 Jesus answered,

"Friend, do the thing you came to do."

Then the men came and grabbed Jesus and arrested him. 51 When that happened, one of Jesus' followers

reached for his sword and pulled it out.

The follower struck the servant of the high priest with the sword and cut off his ear. 52 Jesus said to the man,

"Put your sword back in its place. All who use swords will be killed with swords. 53 Surely you know I could ask my Father, and he would give me more than 12 armies of angels. 54 But this thing must happen this way so that it will be as the Scriptures[d] say."

Matthew 26:55-63

55 Then Jesus said to the crowd,

"You came to get me with swords and clubs as if I were a criminal. Every day I sat in the Temple[d] teaching. You did not arrest me there. 56 But all these things have happened so that it will be as the prophets[d] wrote."

Then all of Jesus' followers left him and ran away.

Jesus Before the Leaders

57 Those men who arrested Jesus led him to the house of Caiaphas, the high priest. The teachers of the law and the Jewish elders were gathered there.

58 Peter followed Jesus but did not go near him. He followed Jesus to the courtyard of the high priest's house. He sat down with the guards to see what would happen to Jesus.

59 The leading priests and the Jewish council tried to find something false against Jesus so that they could kill him. 60 Many people came and told lies about him.

But the council could find no real reason to kill Jesus. Then two people came and said,

61 "This man said, 'I can destroy the Temple[d] of God and build it again in three days.' "

62 Then the high priest stood up and said to Jesus,

"Aren't you going to answer? Don't you have something to say about their charges against you?"

63 But Jesus said nothing.

Again the high priest said to Jesus,

"You must swear to this. I command you by the power of the living God to tell us the truth. Tell us, are you the Christ,[d] the Son of God?"

64 Jesus answered,

"Yes, I am. But I tell you, in the future you will see the Son of Man[d] sitting at the right hand of God, the Powerful One. And you will see him coming in clouds in the sky."

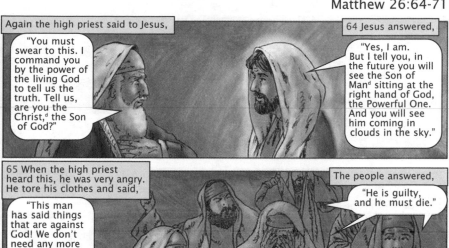

65 When the high priest heard this, he was very angry. He tore his clothes and said,

"This man has said things that are against God! We don't need any more witnesses. You all heard him say these things against God. 66 What do you think?"

The people answered,

"He is guilty, and he must die."

67 Then the people there spit in Jesus' face and beat him with their fists. Others slapped Jesus. 68 They said,

"Prove to us that you are a prophet,[d] you Christ! Tell us who hit you!"

Peter Says He Doesn't Know Jesus

69 At that time, Peter was sitting in the courtyard.

A servant girl came to him and said,

"You were with Jesus, that man from Galilee."

70 But Peter said that he was never with Jesus. He said this to all the people there. Peter said,

"I don't know what you are talking about."

71 Then he left the court-yard. At the gate, another girl saw him. She said to the people there,

"This man was with Jesus of Nazareth."

87

72 Again, Peter said that he was never with Jesus. Peter said,

"I swear that I don't know this man Jesus!"

73 A short time later, some people standing there went to Peter. They said,

"We know you are one of those men who followed Jesus. We know this because of the way you talk."

74 Then Peter began to curse. He said,

"May a curse fall on me if I'm not telling the truth. I don't know the man."

After Peter said this, a rooster crowed. 75 Then he remembered what Jesus had told him: "Before the rooster crows, you will say three times that you don't know me." Then Peter went outside and cried painfully.

Chapter 27

Jesus Is Taken to Pilate

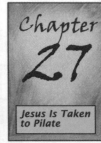

1 Early the next morning, all the leading priests and elders of the people decided to kill Jesus. 2 They tied him, led him away, and turned him over to Pilate, the governor.

Judas Kills Himself

3 Judas saw that they had decided to kill Jesus. Judas was the one who gave Jesus to his enemies. When Judas saw what happened, he was very sorry for what he had done. So he took the 30 silver coins back to the priests and the leaders. 4 Judas said,

"I sinned. I gave you an innocent man to be killed."

The leaders answered,

"What is that to us? That's your problem, not ours."

5 So Judas threw the money into the Temple.[d]

Then he went off and hanged himself.

6 The leading priests picked up the silver coins in the Temple. They said,

"Our law does not allow us to keep this money with the Temple money. This money has paid for a man's death."

7 So they decided to use the coins to buy a field called Potter's Field. This field would be a place to bury strangers who died while visiting Jerusalem.

8 That is why that field is still called the Field of Blood. 9 So the thing came true that Jeremiah the prophet[u] had said: "They took 30 silver coins. That is how little the Israelites thought he was worth. 10 They used those 30 silver coins to buy the potter's field, as the Lord commanded me."[n]

Pilate Questions Jesus

11 Jesus stood before Pilate the governor. Pilate asked him,

"Are you the King of the Jews?"

Jesus answered,

"Yes, I am."

12 When the leading priests and the elders accused Jesus, he said nothing. 13 So Pilate said to Jesus,

"Don't you hear these people accusing you of all these things?"

14 But Jesus said nothing in answer to Pilate. Pilate was very surprised at this.

Pilate Tries to Free Jesus

15 Every year at the time of Passover[d] the governor would free one person from prison. This was always a person the people wanted to be set free. 16 At that time there was a man in prison who was known to be very bad. His name was Barabbas.[n] 17 All the people gathered at Pilate's house. Pilate said,

"Which man do you want me to free: Barabbas,[n] or Jesus who is called the Christ?"[d]

27:9-10 "They . . . commanded me." See Zechariah 11:12-13 and Jeremiah 32:6-9.
27:16, 17 Barabbas Some Greek copies read "Jesus Barabbas."

Matthew 27:18-25

18 Pilate knew that they gave Jesus to him because they were jealous.
19 Pilate said these things while he was sitting on the judge's seat. While he was sitting there, his wife sent a message to him. The message said,

"Don't do anything to that man. He is not guilty. Today I had a dream about him, and it troubled me very much."

20 But the leading priests and elders told the crowd to ask for Barabbas to be freed and for Jesus to be killed.

21 Pilate said,

"I have Barabbas and Jesus. Which do you want me to set free for you?"

They all answered,

"Kill him on a cross!"

The people answered,

"Barabbas!

22 Pilate asked,

"What should I do with Jesus, the one called the Christ?"

23 Pilate asked,

"Why do you want me to kill him? What wrong has he done?"

But they shouted louder,

"Kill him on a cross!"

24 Pilate saw that he could do nothing about this, and a riot was starting. So he took some water and washed his hands[n] in front of the crowd. Then he said,

"I am not guilty of this man's death. You are the ones who are causing it!"

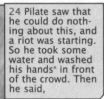

25 All the people answered,

"We will be responsible. We accept for ourselves and for our children any punishment for his death."

27:24 washed his hands He did this as a sign to show that he wanted no part in what the people did.

90

26 Then Pilate freed Barabbas. Pilate told some of the soldiers to beat Jesus with whips. Then he gave Jesus to the soldiers to be killed on a cross.

27 Pilate's soldiers took Jesus into the governor's palace. All the soldiers gathered around Jesus. 28 They took off his clothes and put a red robe on him. 29 Then the soldiers used thorny branches to make a crown. They put this crown of thorns on Jesus' head. They put a stick in his right hand. Then the soldiers bowed before Jesus and made fun of him. They said,

"Hail, King of the Jews!"

Jesus Is Killed on a Cross

30 They spit on Jesus. Then they took his stick and hit him on the head many times. 31 After they finished making fun of Jesus, the soldiers took off the robe and put his own clothes on him again. Then they led Jesus away to be killed on a cross.

32 The soldiers were going out of the city with Jesus. They forced another man to carry the cross to be used for Jesus. This man was Simon, from Cyrene.

33 They all came to the place called Golgotha. (Golgotha means the Place of the Skull.)

34 At Golgotha, the soldiers gave Jesus wine to drink. This wine was mixed with gall.[n] He tasted the wine but refused to drink it.

27:34 gall Probably a drink of wine mixed with drugs to help a person feel less pain.

35 The soldiers nailed Jesus to a cross. They threw lots[d] to decide who would get his clothes.[n]

36 The soldiers sat there and continued watching him. 37 They put a sign above Jesus' head with the charge against him written on it. The sign read: "THIS IS JESUS THE KING OF THE JEWS." 38 Two robbers were nailed to crosses beside Jesus, one on the right and the other on the left. 39 People walked by and insulted Jesus. They shook their heads, 40 saying,

"You said you could destroy the Temple[d] and build it again in three days. So save yourself! Come down from that cross, if you are really the Son of God!"

41 The leading priests, the teachers of the law, and the Jewish elders were also there. These men made fun of Jesus 42 and said,

"He saved other people, but he can't save himself! People say he is the King of Israel! If he is the King, then let him come down now from the cross. Then we will believe in him. 43 He trusts in God. So let God save him now, if God really wants him. He himself said, 'I am the Son of God.' "

27:35 clothes Some Greek copies continue, "So what God said through the prophet came true, 'They divided my clothes among them, and they threw lots for my clothing.' "

44 And in the same way, the robbers who were being killed on crosses beside Jesus also insulted him.

Jesus Dies

45 At noon the whole country became dark. This darkness lasted for three hours. 46 About three o'clock Jesus cried out in a loud voice,

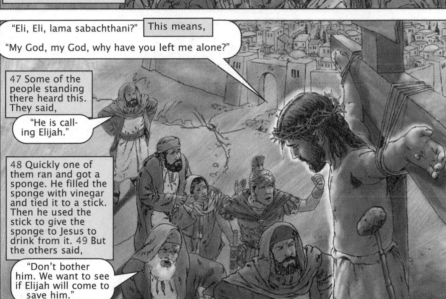

"Eli, Eli, lama sabachthani?" This means,

"My God, my God, why have you left me alone?"

47 Some of the people standing there heard this. They said,

"He is calling Elijah."

48 Quickly one of them ran and got a sponge. He filled the sponge with vinegar and tied it to a stick. Then he used the stick to give the sponge to Jesus to drink from it. 49 But the others said,

"Don't bother him. We want to see if Elijah will come to save him."

50 Again Jesus cried out in a loud voice. Then he died.
51 Then the curtain in the Temple[n] split into two pieces. The tear started at the top and tore all the way down to the bottom. Also, the earth shook and rocks broke apart. 52 The graves opened, and many of God's people who had died were raised from death.
53 They came out of the graves after Jesus was raised from death. They went into the holy city, and many people saw them.

27:51 curtain in the Temple A curtain divided the Most Holy Place from the other part of the Temple. That was the special building in Jerusalem where God commanded the Jews to worship him.

54 The army officer and the soldiers guarding Jesus saw this earthquake and everything else that happened. They were very frightened and said,

"He really was the Son of God!"

55 Many women were standing at a distance from the cross, watching. These were women who had followed Jesus from Galilee to care for him. 56 Mary Magdalene, and Mary the mother of James and Joseph, and the mother of James and John were there.

Jesus Is Buried

57 That evening a rich man named Joseph came to Jerusalem. He was a follower of Jesus from the town of Arimathea. 58 Joseph went to Pilate and asked to have Jesus' body. Pilate gave orders for the soldiers to give it to Joseph.

59 Then Joseph took the body and wrapped it in a clean linen cloth.

60 He put Jesus' body in a new tomb that he had cut in a wall of rock. He rolled a very large stone to block the entrance of the tomb. Then Joseph went away.

61 Mary Magdalene and the other woman named Mary were sitting near the tomb.

The Tomb of Jesus Is Guarded

62 That day was the day called Preparation[d] Day. The next day, the leading priests and the Pharisees[d] went to Pilate. 63 They said,

"Sir, we remember that while that liar was still alive he said, 'After three days I will rise from death.' 64 So give the order for the tomb to be guarded closely till the third day. His followers might come and steal the body. Then they could tell the people that he has risen from death. That lie would be even worse than the first one."

65 Pilate said,

"Take some soldiers and go guard the tomb the best way you know."

66 So they all went to the tomb and made it safe from thieves. They did this by sealing the stone in the entrance and then putting soldiers there to guard it.

chapter
28

Jesus Rises from Death

1 The day after the Sabbath[d] day was the first day of the week. At dawn on the first day, Mary Magdalene and another woman named Mary went to look at the tomb. 2 At that time there was a strong earthquake. An angel of the Lord came down from heaven. The angel went to the tomb and rolled the stone away from the entrance. Then he sat on the stone. 3 He was shining as bright as lightning. His clothes were white as snow. 4 The soldiers guarding the tomb were very frightened of the angel. They shook with fear and then became like dead men.

5 The angel said to the women,

"Don't be afraid. I know that you are looking for Jesus, the one who was killed on the cross. 6 But he is not here. He has risen from death as he said he would. Come and see the place where his body was. 7 And go quickly and tell his followers. Say to them: 'Jesus has risen from death. He is going into Galilee. He will be there before you. You will see him there.' " Then the angel said, "Now I have told you."

8 The women left the tomb quickly. They were afraid, but they were also very happy. They ran to tell Jesus' followers what had happened.

9 Suddenly, Jesus met them and said, "Greetings." The women came up to Jesus, took hold of his feet, and worshiped him. 10 Then Jesus said to them,

"Don't be afraid. Go and tell my brothers to go on to Galilee. They will see me there."

The Soldiers Report to the Jewish Leaders

11 The women went to tell Jesus' followers. At the same time, some of the soldiers who had been guarding the tomb went into the city. They went to tell the leading priests everything that had happened. 12 Then the priests met with the Jewish elders and made a plan. They paid the soldiers a large amount of money. 13 They said to the soldiers,

"Tell the people that Jesus' followers came during the night and stole the body while you were asleep. 14 If the governor hears about this, we will satisfy him and save you from trouble."

15 So the soldiers kept the money and obeyed the priests. And that story is still spread among the Jews even today.

Jesus Talks to His Followers

16 The 11 followers went to Galilee. They went to the mountain where Jesus told them to go. 17 On the mountain they saw Jesus and worshiped him. But some of them did not believe that it was really Jesus. 18 Then Jesus came to them and said,

"All power in heaven and on earth is given to me. 19 So go and make followers of all people in the world. Baptize them in the name of the Father and the Son and the Holy Spirit.[d] 20 Teach them to obey everything that I have told you. You can be sure that I will be with you always. I will continue with you until the end of the world."

People I Want
to Pray For

Situations
I Want to Pray For

_____   _____
_____   _____
_____   _____
_____   _____
_____   _____
_____   _____
_____   _____
_____   _____
_____   _____
_____   _____
_____   _____
_____   _____
_____   _____
_____   _____
_____   _____
_____   _____
_____   _____
_____   _____

Answered
Prayers

_____   _____
_____   _____
_____   _____
_____   _____
_____   _____
_____   _____
_____   _____
_____   _____
_____   _____
_____   _____
_____   _____
_____   _____
_____   _____
_____   _____
_____   _____
_____   _____
_____   _____
_____   _____
_____   _____
_____   _____
_____   _____

Notes